"James White says *The Church in an Age of C*
'a whirlwind tour of our day that is meant to introduce and provoke.'
The author has succeeded. This book is hard-hitting as well as carefully researched. It is also extremely relevant for our day. In twenty-five concise chapters, White scans the landscape of the postmodern world we now live in, especially in America and Western culture. This book will serve the church well."

Daniel L. Akin, president, Southeastern Baptist
Theological Seminary

"*The Church in an Age of Crisis* is more than a survey of the cultural landscape of contemporary America. It is a call to bring Christian values to bear in the marketplace of ideas. With prophetic insight, James Emery White directs the church to be true to its calling—to be salt and light in a dying world."

Alec Hill, president, InterVarsity Christian Fellowship USA

"This book is a wake-up call for those who really care about America and how lost so many are today. There's enough analysis of the spiritual confusion of our time to break your heart. The popular song from twenty years ago, 'Losing My Religion,' sums up where so many of our fellow citizens are. But *The Church in an Age of Crisis* provides positive answers on how the grace of God in Christ can break through even the stoniest of hearts."

Jerry Newcombe, Truth in Action Ministries

"Dr. White has given believers a most valuable gift here. The church indeed finds itself at the dawn of the seventh age, a time very similar to what Paul experienced at the Areopagus. He knew what message was needed. White gives sage insight and direction in wisely engaging this age with the wisdom of Paul as well as the discernment of the honorable sons of Issachar. This book is essential for those who desire to bring the truth, love, and light of Christ to our challenging present age."

Glenn T. Stanton, director, Global Family Formation Studies and
Ministry Strategy Development, Focus on the Family

THE
CHURCH
IN AN AGE OF
CRISIS

(25) | New Realities
Facing Christianity

JAMES EMERY WHITE

BakerBooks

a division of Baker Publishing Group
Grand Rapids, Michigan

Published by Baker Books
a division of Baker Publishing Group
P.O. Box 6287, Grand Rapids, MI 49516-6287
www.bakerbooks.com

Printed in the United States of America

Library of Congress Cataloging-in-Publication Data
White, James Emery, 1961–
    The church in an age of crisis : 25 new realities facing Christianity / James Emery White.
        p.   cm.
    Includes bibliographical references (p.   ).
    ISBN 978-0-8010-1387-4 (pbk.)
    1. Christianity and culture—History—21st century. 2. Christianity—21st century. I. Title.
BR115.C8W45 2012
270.8′3—dc23   2012022208

Unless otherwise indicated, Scripture quotations are from the Holy Bible, New International Version®. NIV®. Copyright © 1973, 1978, 1984, 2011 by Biblica, Inc.™ Used by permission of Zondervan. All rights reserved worldwide. www.zondervan.com

Scripture quotations labeled ASV are from the American Standard Version of the Bible.

Scripture quotations labeled Message are from *The Message* by Eugene H. Peterson, copyright © 1993, 1994, 1995, 2000, 2001, 2002. Used by permission of NavPress Publishing Group. All rights reserved.

Scripture quotations labeled NLT are from the *Holy Bible*, New Living Translation, copyright © 1996, 2004, 2007 by Tyndale House Foundation. Used by permission of Tyndale House Publishers, Inc., Carol Stream, Illinois 60188. All rights reserved.

The internet addresses, email addresses, and phone numbers in this book are accurate at the time of publication. They are provided as a resource. Baker Publishing Group does not endorse them or vouch for their content or permanence.

In keeping with biblical principles of creation stewardship, Baker Publishing Group advocates the responsible use of our natural resources. As a member of the Green Press Initiative, our company uses recycled paper when possible. The text paper of this book is composed in part of post-consumer waste.

12 13 14 15 16 17 18   7 6 5 4 3 2 1

Contents

Marriage and Family

Media and Technology

Mission

Acknowledgments

I wish to thank the Baker team for their support of this project, specifically Bob Hosack. I was given great freedom and extended great patience in developing this, for which I am most grateful.

Glynn Goble keeps my life ordered so I can write; Alli Main helps me be a better writer and frees me up in so many ways; and my wife, Susan, continues to make every page possible.

Introduction

A Seventh Age

The city of Middelburg in the southwestern Netherlands dates back to the late eighth century, and to this day it remains a quiet little town of less than 50,000 inhabitants. But two inventions, within a handful of years of each other, burst from this island city's cobblestone streets and changed the world. One allows human beings to gaze far away across vast distances; the other allows us to peer deeply into that which most closely surrounds us.

"We are certain," Galileo wrote in 1623, "the first inventor of the telescope was a simple spectacle-maker."[1] Historian Daniel Boorstin notes that the most likely story places the event in the shop of an obscure Dutch craftsman named Hans Lippershey in Middelburg about 1600. In the hands of Galileo, and turned toward the heavens, our view of the world—and of our place in the cosmos—was forever changed. Meanwhile, Zacharias Jansen, another spectacle-maker from Middelburg, stumbled on a device that opened another world to the human eye: the microscope. As Galileo seized on the invention of the telescope to chart the galaxies, Antoni van Leeuwenhoek took advantage of the development of the microscope to explore the equally vast world of the miniscule.[2]

From one city came two inventions that offered radically different vistas, supplying much-needed perspectives on the complexity and depth of our universe. One allowed a look at the world around us, the other a look at the world within.

We need such tools today, not for the cosmos, much less the inner world of the microbe, but for our culture. Culture is perhaps best defined as the world in which we live and the world that lives in us.

But is it a world we understand?

The Men of Issachar

I have long been intrigued by an obscure passage in the Old Testament Scriptures, almost a throwaway comment, about a group of men within the people of Israel. They were known as the men of Issachar.

We don't know much about them. Issachar himself was the fifth son of Jacob and Leah and the ninth son overall for the patriarch. The name itself seems to derive from the joining of the Hebrew word for *man* and the Hebrew word for *wages*, thus a "hired man" or "hired worker." He had four sons, and he went with his father into Egypt, where he died and was buried. Afterward his descendants formed one of the tribes of Israel. By the end of the wanderings of Israel through the Sinai desert, they numbered over 60,000 fighting men. When the Promised Land was apportioned, the men of Issachar received sixteen cities and their adjoining villages. Moses referred to them as a "strong ass" situated in a beautiful land (Gen. 49:14 ASV). It was a compliment.

They were quick to follow one of their own, the great female judge Deborah, into battle to break the stronghold the Canaanites held over their lives. A minor judge, Tola, was also among their number, as were two kings: Baasha and his son, Elah. When Solomon established the twelve administrative districts of Israel, Issachar's territory became one of those independent provinces. In the book of Revelation, the tribe of Issachar is again mentioned where the 12,000 were sealed (Rev. 7:1–8).

What is most evident is that by the time of David, the men of Issachar, then numbering nearly 90,000, were known supremely for their wisdom. It was later noted in the Talmud that the wisest members of the Sanhedrin came from the men of Issachar. But theirs was not just any wisdom; it was a specific kind of wisdom: "From the tribe of Issachar, there were 200 leaders. . . . All these men understood the signs of the times and knew the best course for Israel to take" (1 Chron. 12:32, NLT).

That's the comment that has always captured my attention. They knew the "signs of the times" *and* how best to live in light of them.

What a powerful and important combination. To know the signs of the times is more than headlines and tweets; it is knowing what is significant among the happenings of our world—events and movements, trends and ideologies. It is being keenly aware of the dynamics of culture that are consequential.

And how.

And why.

But that's not all. The men of Issachar didn't simply know those signs; they knew how to then live in light of them. They had a sense of what to think, how to act, and the manner in which to respond. Real wisdom is always more than knowledge; it is living *according* to that knowledge in the most appropriate way.

Knowing the signs of the times and how then to live has never been more pressing. In his *Memoirs*, Jean-Francois Paul de Gondi, Cardinal de Retz, writes, "*Il n'y a rien dans le monde qui n'ait son moment decisif.*" "There is nothing in the world which does not have its decisive moment."[3]

There is little doubt that in our world, at this time, we have reached our decisive moment.

A Seventh Age

During my time at Oxford, I was introduced to a historian by the name of Christopher Dawson, who penned one of the more intriguing observations about the flow of history.[4] Dawson suggested that there have been six identifiable *ages* in relation to the Christian church, each lasting for three or four centuries and each following a similar course.

Each age began and then ended in crisis. The heart of each crisis was an intense attack by new enemies, within and without the church, which in turn demanded new spiritual determination and drive. Without this determination and drive, the church would have lost the day.

Dawson accounted for six such ages at the time of his writing. It is my belief that we are now entering a seventh.[5]

The crisis itself, of course, is quite apparent. Consider the past decade, 2000–2009. It started with the fear and worry of the Y2K millennium bug that we thought would crash computers, crash planes, and crash the infrastructure. Little did we know that the real horror associated with "2" would involve the destruction of towers, not computers. There followed a war in Iraq and then a war in Afghanistan. Then just when many felt hope had arrived through the historic election of the nation's first African-American president, the worst economic meltdown since the Great Depression reared its ugly head. What started with the dot-com bubble and Enron ended with the mortgage and stock market crisis. It's understandable that *Billboard* magazine named Daniel Powter's "Bad Day"—which reigned on top of the *Billboard* pop charts for five weeks in 2006—the decade's top one-hit wonder.[6] Throw in Abu Ghraib, Virginia Tech, and Fort Hood, and it's no surprise that the editors of *Time* magazine have called it "The Decade from Hell."[7] This assessment has settled deeply into our psyche. A *Wall Street Journal*/NBC News poll on the eve of 2012 found that a staggering 73 percent of all Americans believe we as a nation are on the wrong track.[8]

I agree. I have no idea whether this seventh age is the last age or one of many ages yet to come. But I do know that this is *our* day and hour, and we must meet the demands of its challenge.

The World before a Watching Church

We are living at the beginning of our future. The world is changing, and we need to recognize the nature of that change. The seismic shifts in culture will change the world's attitude toward Christ and decisively challenge those who follow him.

This book offers a whirlwind tour of our day that is meant to introduce and provoke. Each chapter could be a book unto itself, and many good works have explored their ideas in depth. But there comes a time for a survey—a primer of sorts—on the world in which we live and the world that lives in us. Many of the signs are disturbing, but we ignore them at great peril, for it was knowledge of just such signs that afforded the men of Issachar the decisive advantage of being able to know what to do.

I do not attempt to offer all of the answers in this work. I've ventured a few ideas in previous writings, but here I focus on knowing the signs themselves, gathered under the headings of faith, mindset, marriage and family, media and technology, and mission. It has been said that we, as a church, live before a watching world. In doing so, we must also understand the world as a watching church. I hope this book will help open our eyes.

Which means opening them to our times.

FAITH

1

A Post-Christian America

While the South is hardly Christ-centered, it is most
certainly Christ-haunted.

Flannery O'Connor[1]

A couple of years ago a film crew from our church hit the streets
of Charlotte, North Carolina, to produce a "person on the street"
video asking people, "What comes to your mind when you think of
the Christmas story?"

Number one answer?

"The movie."

Yep, the 1983 "You'll shoot your eye out, kid" tale from 1940s Indiana of a nine-year-old boy's desire for a Red Ryder Carbon-Action
200-Shot Range Model Air Rifle BB Gun (and, lest we forget, with a
compass in the stock).

An intriguing editorial in *Time* magazine at around the same time
chronicled how *A Christmas Story* had become the quintessential
American film for Christmas, replacing *It's a Wonderful Life*. Titled
"Generation X-Mas," the editorial chronicled how an "upstart film
became a holiday icon for the post-boomer set."

As for George Bailey? "Not so into him anymore."

Those from older generations picked Bedford Falls, along with Macy's (*Miracle on 34ᵗʰ Street*) as their favorite film destinations. But respondents a bit younger, from eighteen to forty-one years old, granted the major award to Scott Fargas, Flick, and the Bumpus's dogs.

Time suggested this as one of the pop-cultural shifts, such as football overtaking baseball and salsa defeating ketchup, that signal bigger changes. Perhaps this is because *A Christmas Story* is everything *It's a Wonderful Life* is not: "satiric and myth-deflating, down to the cranky store Santa kicking Ralphie down a slide." Or perhaps it is because of the changing relationship between the community and the individual. Whereas the older films position Christmas as that which "uplifts the suicidal, raises every voice in Whoville, [and] renders peace between Macy and Gimbel," *A Christmas Story* "inverts the moral."[2]

Now it's the individual Christmas experience that matters. Getting the BB gun, instead of protecting the local Savings and Loan for the poor, is the point. Or as *Time* put it, "It's the individual Christmas that matters. Bedford Falls can take a hike . . . [it's not about] angels getting their wings. Christmas is about the kids getting their due."[3]

But perhaps we can go where *Time* could not. The great divide between *It's a Wonderful Life* and *A Christmas Story* is more than just the radical individualism that marks our day; it is what spawned such individualism. The real divide between the two films is that one retains the idea that Christmas is about the birth of the Christ child and one does not. Unless I have missed it, *A Christmas Story* does not have a single reference, symbol, picture, or event that suggests Christmas is about the birth of Christ or has religious significance of any kind. There is a brief snippet of "Go Tell It on the Mountain," but that's about it.

It's a Wonderful Life, on the other hand, is rich in Christian ideas and ethos, from traditional Christmas songs celebrating the birth of Christ (the climax of the movie is marked by the spontaneous outburst of "Hark the Herald Angels Sing") to the central character of an angel. *A Christmas Story* is marked by the total absence of anything religious, much less Christian. No nativity scenes, no church services, no Christian music—even Higbee's department store honors the season not with shepherds or wise men but with characters from *The Wizard of Oz*.

Yet this reflects more than the choice of one movie over another. An analysis of 48,000 hours of programming by the NRB (National Religious Broadcasters) found that 90 percent of holiday programming did not have a significant spiritual theme; 7 percent had a religious or spiritual theme but did not refer to Jesus or the biblical story of his birth. Jesus was the focus of only 3 percent of all Christmas programming.[4]

I'll confess that *A Christmas Story* has become one of my favorite movies. The nostalgia of the time and the way it reveals how Christmas often works runs deep and familiar. But when I watch it, along with millions of others, I remind myself that while it is *a* Christmas story, it is not *the* Christmas story.

But it is for our nation.

And more than our Christmas narrative, it reflects the new state of faith.

The most foundational understanding of the culture of our Western world and the future that it portends is that it is increasingly post-Christian. By post-Christian, I do not mean non-Christian. I do not mean anti-Christian. I mean we live in a country that is increasingly losing any memory of what it means to even *be* Christian.

The Twilight of Atheism and the Dawn of Secularism

A 2004 survey of religion and politics sponsored by the Pew Forum on Religion and Public Life found only 7.5 percent of the American population self-categorized themselves as *secularists*. But columnist David Klinghoffer maintains that those embracing secularism far exceed the 7.5 percent figure because many individuals who identify nominally as Jews or Christians are, in fact, devout secularists.[5]

The idea of a secularist is important. Much is often made about atheism, but atheism is not at the heart of the much more robust and pervasive secularism. The heart of the secular religion is moral relativism, a *functional* atheism, if you will, that holds that how life is to be lived is dictated by a particular situation in light of a particular culture or social location. Though there may be a higher power, that higher power is not fleshed out in terms of authority. As a result, moral values become a matter of personal opinion or private judgment rather than something grounded in objective truth.[6]

So rather than rejecting the idea of God, secular religion simply ignores him. We function independent of any transcendent referent. This has created a "spiritual without being religious" mentality that sounds very good on the surface but translates into a veneer of spirituality that is without content and is filled with little more than our personal meaning. Paul M. Zulehner, dean of Vienna University's divinity school and one of the world's most distinguished sociologists of religion, maintains that a "false spirituality" is rising that will prove to be "a more dangerous rival to the Christian faith than atheism."[7]

Alarmist thinking?

Not after this most revealing study on American faith in recent history.

A Land of Swedes

The headlines were arresting:

> "Almost All Denominations Losing Ground: Faith Is Shifting, Drifting or Vanishing Outright" (*USA Today*)
>
> "We're Losing Our Religion" (*Associated Press*)
>
> "America Becoming Less Christian" (CNN)
>
> "US Religion ID Inching to 'None'" (*Seattle Times*)
>
> "None of Thee Above" (*Religious News Service*)[8]

The headlines come from the American Religious Identification Survey (ARIS) released on March 9, 2009. Much in the study was to be expected: mainline denominations are losing ground; the Bible Belt is less Baptist; Catholics have invaded the South; denominationalism as a whole is on the wane.

What was most alarming was the increase in those who said they had no religion—nearly doubling from 8 percent to 15 percent, making those who claim no religion at all the third largest defined constituency in the United States, eclipsed only by Catholics and Baptists. Further, they were the only religious bloc to rise in percentage in every single state, thus constituting the only truly national trend.

As the ARIS report concluded, "The challenge to Christianity . . . does not come from other religions but from a rejection of all forms of organized religion."[9] Barry Kosmin, coresearcher for the survey, warned against blaming atheism for driving up the percentage of Americans who say they have no religion. "They're not thinking about religion and rejecting it; they're not thinking about it at all."[10]

Simply put, supposedly "Christian" America has become a mission field.

But not just any mission field. When it comes to the United States, think Sweden. Sociologist Phil Zuckerman chronicled his fourteen months investigating Danes and Swedes about religion, concluding that religion "wasn't really so much a private, personal issue, but rather, a non-issue." His interviewees just didn't care about it. As one replied, "I really have never thought about that. . . . It's been fun to get these kinds of questions that I never, never think about."[11] Years earlier, another sociologist, Peter Berger, quipped, "If India is the most religious country on our planet, and Sweden is the least religious, America is a land of Indians ruled by Swedes."[12]

Now we are increasingly simply Swedes.

The Dilemma of Denial

An online poll conducted by AOL soon after the selection of Cardinal Joseph Ratzinger to be the next pope revealed what people perceived to be Pope Benedict XVI's greatest challenges. Sanctity of life issues, such as cloning or stem cells, came in first, followed by the priest shortage. Distant on the list was the rise of secularism.

Fortunately, the new pope does not seem driven by polls. He exhibits a sound awareness of secularism's threat, wisely discerning that sanctity of life issues, along with the priest shortage, are the *symptoms* of secularism's rise.[13] Benedict XVI had a ringside seat to secularism's deadly effects in Western Europe and specifically his German homeland. Today fewer than one of every ten Germans worships even once a month, and a majority of Germans and other Northern Europeans confess that God does not matter to them at all.

Little wonder that in Ratzinger's pre-election sermon to his fellow cardinals he made the following declaration: "A dictatorship of relativism is being formed, one that recognizes nothing as definitive and that has as its measure only the self and its desires."[14]

Unlike the pope's assessment of his homeland, most American Christians are in denial. They insist that America is a Christian nation by origin and that it still largely functions as one.

When America's second president, John Adams, and America's third president, Thomas Jefferson, both died on the same day in 1826—and that day being none other than the Fourth of July—it was seen as a sign of God's favor on the United States. As historian David McCullough notes in his widely acclaimed biography of Adams, it "could not be seen as mere coincidence: it was a 'visible and palpable' manifestation of 'Divine favor,' wrote John Quincy in his diary that night, expressing what was felt and would be said again and again everywhere the news spread."[15]

The idea of being a chosen nation and receiving special blessing from God has been a constant theme throughout the history of the United States, beginning with the Puritans and their "city on a shining hill."[16] In more recent times, the vision of a Christian America was popularized in the late 1970s by authors Peter Marshall and David Manuel in *The Light and the Glory*. Marshall and Manuel held that America was founded as a Christian nation and flourished under the benevolent hand of divine providence, arguing further that America's blessings will remain only as long as America as a nation is faithful to God.[17] In 1989 a team of evangelical historians (Mark Noll, Nathan Hatch, and George Marsden) attempted to lay this rather dubious thesis to rest, but it continues as a popular framework among contemporary American evangelicals for viewing American history.[18]

Even if one chooses to believe we were founded as an explicitly Christian nation under the divine hand of God's favor, we have clearly chosen to depart from our calling. But as long as an exalted view of America's current adherence to the Christian faith remains in force, the true nature of the challenge will not be addressed.

And it is a challenge that *must* be met.

America is not simply the leader of the modern world; it is the principal carrier of globalization and exporter of culture. I believe the ideas that lie at the heart of the West, and particularly the United States, are Judeo-Christian. Yet America is at great spiritual risk. This has rightly led some to call for a third mission to the West before all is lost.[19]

The first mission was the apostolic mission that eventually resulted in the conversion of the people of the Roman Empire. The second mission followed the fall of Rome as missionaries refounded Western civilization and essentially reconverted the West back to Christianity from paganism—what Thomas Cahill refers to in the title of his book *How the Irish Saved Civilization*. A third mission should seek to restore America as the leader of the Western world and to her Judeo-Christian roots, ensuring continued vibrancy and influence for years to come.

Missions to the West

First Mission: The apostolic mission eventually resulted in the conversion of the Roman Empire.

Second Mission: Missionaries refounded Western civilization and essentially reconverted the West back to Christianity from paganism.

Third Mission: This movement should seek to restore America as the leader of the Western world and to her Judeo-Christian roots.

It is difficult to think of America as a mission field, having been the exporter of faith for so many generations. But that is precisely what it has become. If the first American Revolution was fought to free ourselves from political tyranny, a second revolution is now needed to liberate ourselves from spiritual lethargy. And that would be an American revolution worth fighting for, even more than the first.

2

Why Johnny Can't Pray

There is no longer a Christian mind.

Harry Blamires[1]

Every week we encourage people attending our church to turn in a connection card to request information about the church or to explore next steps. A staff person then contacts them and attempts to serve in any way needed. One of our staff members recently received an email from a woman following a connection card response. This is what she wrote:

> Thanks for the informative email. I have been going to Meck for about a month now and I love it! I have even talked my two friends into joining. We are all thankful to be part of an awesome church with great values. I do have one question. I remember hearing about . . . [an upcoming] celebration of the Lord's Supper. *What does that mean? . . . What is a celebration of the Lord's Supper? Does that mean we all bring some kind of food to share?* I am planning on going . . . but I wanted to make sure I bring something if need be. Any information you can provide . . . would be greatly appreciated!

Soak that in.

An announcement about the celebration of the Lord's Supper made her wonder if she needed to bring coleslaw.

I don't know about you, but I think Jesus is really, really fond of this person and loves all that she doesn't know and is excited about her journey. And as a pastor, I am overwhelmed that God trusts me with such people. In fact, our church experiences over 70 percent of its total growth from the unchurched, and I thank God for that daily. But in truth, this is not a situation unique to a church that is reaching the unchurched because this woman is far from alone.

When it comes to Christianity, people just don't know much.

Only 19 percent of all Protestants know that salvation comes through faith alone, not by works. And 45 percent cannot name the four Gospels. Only 55 percent know that the Golden Rule is not one of the Ten Commandments.[2] An Episcopalian priest from South Carolina said, "A couple came into my office once with a yellow pad of their teenage son's questions. One of them was: 'What is that guy doing hanging up there on the plus sign?'"

And these are the people *in* the church.

Failing the Test

For the last several years, Stephen Prothero, chairman of the religion department of Boston University, has administered a fifteen-question quiz to his undergraduate students—one they consistently fail.[3]

It includes such questions as:

- Name the four Gospels.
- According to the Bible, where was Jesus born?
- President George W. Bush spoke in his first inaugural address of the Jericho road. What Bible story was he invoking?
- What are the first five books of the Hebrew Bible or the Christian Old Testament?
- What is the Golden Rule?
- "God helps those who help themselves." Is this in the Bible? If so, where?
- "Blessed are the poor in spirit, for theirs is the kingdom of God." Does this appear in the Bible?
- Name the Ten Commandments.

Needless to say, most of his students don't have a clue.

But it's not just an absence of knowing what is or is not in the Bible; it's having what we *think* we know be wrong as well.

Did You Pass the Test?

1. The four Gospels are Matthew, Mark, Luke, and John.

2. Jesus was born in Bethlehem of Judea.

3. The parable of the Good Samaritan, Luke 10:30–37.

4. Genesis, Exodus, Leviticus, Numbers, and Deuteronomy.

5. The Golden Rule is, "Do to others what you would have them do to you" (Matt. 7:12).

6. "God helps those who help themselves" is not found anywhere in the Bible.

7. It is from the Sermon on the Mount, Matthew 5:3.

8. The Ten Commandments are listed in Exodus 20:1–17.

In a news conference after he was fired as head coach of the Chicago Bears, Mike Ditka decided to quote the Bible. "Scripture tells you that all things shall pass," a choked-up Ditka offered. "This, too, shall pass." The only problem is that "this, too, shall pass" isn't in the Bible. As a recent report by CNN noted, "The Bible may be the most revered book in America, but it's also one of the most misquoted."[4]

Ditka's misquote was a phantom passage, meaning it is quoted as Scripture when it's not actually in the Bible. There are many more. For example:

"God helps those who help themselves."

"God works in mysterious ways."

"Cleanliness is next to godliness."

Not in the Bible.

And then there are verses that are in the Bible but are often misstated. For example, "Spare the rod and spoil the child." That's not in the Bible either, but something close to it is: "Whoever spares the rod hates their children, but the one who loves their children is careful to discipline them" (Prov. 13:24).

There are also times we read things into a passage that really aren't there. For example, take the reference to Satan tempting Eve to eat the forbidden apple in the Garden of Eden. The serpent is never identified as the devil in Genesis, and we are never told that Eve ate an apple. Fruit, yes. But the kind of fruit? We have no idea. The same is true for Jonah and the whale. Big fish? Yep. Whale? It never says. The original Hebrew suggests little more than a large fish.

And the three wise men? It doesn't say three.

This goes beyond matters related to the Bible. It's reflective of an ignorance of Christian faith. And not just Christian faith, but Christian history, Christian thought, and Christians themselves.

Consider the dismissal of vice-presidential candidate Sarah Palin by MSNBC commentator Richard Wolffe for reading C. S. Lewis for "divine inspiration." Appearing on MSNBC's *Hardball* with Chris Matthews, Wolffe reacted with mocking incredulity, noting that Lewis did little more than write "a series of kids' books."

Credit to Matthews who responded, "I wouldn't put down C. S. Lewis."

"I'm not putting him down," Wolffe responded. "But you know divine inspiration? There are things she could've said to divine inspiration. Choosing C. S. Lewis is an interesting one."[5]

This isn't about Palin. It's about Wolffe's ignorance of Lewis. Simply an author of children's books? Lest we forget—and obviously some have—this is the man who, in the words of the *London Times*, "in his own lifetime became a legend."

It seems legends fade fast. At least Christian ones.

Lewis went to University College, Oxford, where he achieved a rare Double First in Classics, an additional First in English, and the Chancellor's Prize for academics. He was soon offered a teaching position at Magdalen College, Oxford, where he was a fellow and tutor from 1925 to 1954, and then at the University of Cambridge as professor of medieval and Renaissance English (1954–1963).

In 1931 Lewis came out of atheism into the Christian faith, aided significantly through his friendship with J. R. R. Tolkien, author of

The Lord of the Rings. The intellectual questions that plagued him during his spiritual journey—why God allows pain and suffering, how Christianity can be the one and only way to God, the existence of miracles—became the very questions he helped others navigate with such skill as a Christian. His first work, *The Pilgrim's Regress: An Allegorical Apology for Christianity, Reason and Romanticism*, came out in 1933. There followed a torrent of works, eventually reaching forty titles, the vast majority attempting to put forward Christianity in a very non-Christian world. Among the more widely known are *The Screwtape Letters*; *Out of the Silent Planet, Perelandra*, and *That Hideous Strength*, a trilogy of science fiction novels (when the genre was hardly known); and yes, the Chronicles of Narnia, a series of seven children's books that are widely heralded as classics of fantasy literature.

It was through a series of radio addresses, given over the BBC during the Second World War but later published in three separate parts, that his conversational style, wit, intellect, and rough charm revealed Christianity to millions. The first invitation from BBC was for four fifteen-minute talks. The response was so overwhelming that they gave him a fifth fifteen-minute segment to answer listeners' questions.

Then a second round of talks were requested and given. The clarity of Lewis's thought, his ability to gather together a wide range of information and make it plain, led one listener to remark that they "were magnificent, unforgettable. Nobody, before or since, has made such an 'impact' in straight talks of this kind."[6]

The BBC asked for a third round of talks, this time stretching out for eight consecutive weeks. Lewis consented, but he made it clear it would be his last. His goal throughout was simple: "I was . . . writing to expound . . . 'mere' Christianity, which is what it is and was what it was long before I was born."[7] Eventually gathered together in a single book titled *Mere Christianity*, the work continues to make Christianity known to millions.

But people's ignorance about someone like Lewis is only a hint of the problem. More recently the bishop of Winchester, the Rt. Rev. Michael Scott-Joynt, warned that the death of religious literacy among those who make and administer the law in the U.K. has created an imbalance in the way in which Christians as a minority are treated when compared to sexual minorities. Consider these examples:

- a Christian counselor was fired for refusing to give sex therapy to a homosexual couple
- Christian bed and breakfast owners were sued for turning away two homosexuals who wished to share a bedroom
- Christian adoption agencies were forced by the government to close their doors after they refused to place children with same-sex couples

The bishop's point is that "for the first time in British history politicians and judges were largely ignorant of religion and so failed to appreciate the importance Christians placed on abiding by the Scriptures rather than the politically correct values of the secular state."[8]

Scott-Joynt's comments to the BBC are worth repeating at length:

> Probably for the first time in our history there is a widespread lack of religious literacy among those who one way and another hold power and influence, whether it's Parliament or the media or even, dare I say it, in the judiciary. The risk would be that there are increasingly professions where it could be difficult for people who are devoted believers to work in certain [areas] of the public services, indeed in Parliament. Anybody who is part of the religious community believes that you don't just hold views, you live them. Manifesting your faith is part of having it and not part of some optional bolt-on. Judgment seemed to be following contemporary society, which seems to think that secularist views are statements of the obvious and religious views are notions in the mind. That is the culture in which we are living. The judges ought to be religiously literate enough to know that there is an argument behind all this, which can't simply be settled by the nature of society as it is today.[9]

It's one thing to be ignorant about the twentieth century's greatest Christian apologist; it's another to be ignorant about the mere Christianity he so faithfully professed and, in turn, persecute Christians who embrace it. One is galling; the other is frightening.

Prothero argues, and rightly so, that everyone needs to grasp Bible basics as well as the core beliefs, stories, symbols, and heroes of other faiths. In a commentary for the *Los Angeles Times* titled "We Live in the Land of Biblical Idiots," Prothero maintains that biblical illiteracy is not just a religious problem, it is a civic problem with political consequences.

> How can citizens participate in biblically inflected debates on abortion, capital punishment, or the environment without knowing something about the Bible? . . . An entire generation of Americans is growing up almost entirely ignorant of the most influential book in world history, unable to understand the 1,300 biblical allusions in Shakespeare, [or] the scriptural oratory of President Lincoln and the Rev. Martin Luther King Jr.[10]

Such admonishments are hardly new. In the late 1980s, E. D. Hirsch burst onto the scene with his idea of "cultural literacy," which detailed the importance of having a core of background knowledge for functional literacy and effective national communication, much of it including religion.[11] In my own *A Mind for God*, I argue for the importance of foundational biblical, historical, and theological literacy and the importance of churches serving the pursuit of such literacy.[12]

Why? As Winston Churchill presciently stated in his address to Harvard University in 1943, "The empires of the future will be empires of the mind." Alister McGrath, reflecting on Churchill's address, notes that Churchill's point was that a great transition was taking place in Western culture with immense implications for all who live in it. The powers of the new world would not be nation-states, as with empires past, but ideologies. It would now be ideas, not nations, that would captivate and conquer in the future. The starting point for the conquest of the world would now be the human mind.[13] As John Stott once noted, "We may talk of 'conquering' the world for Christ. But what sort of 'conquest' do we mean? Not a victory by force of arms. . . . This is a battle of ideas."[14]

But when the ideas inherent within the Christian faith are being lost, they cannot play a role in the life of the Christ-follower, much less in the cultural marketplace.

That's why Johnny can't pray.

He doesn't know how.

3

The Church of the Jedi

The gods of the East are infinite by definition . . .
but they are not personal. The gods of the West were
personal, but they were very limited. The Christian
God, the God of the Bible, is personal-infinite.

Francis A. Schaeffer[1]

In their book *America's Four Gods*, authors Paul Forese and Christopher Bader drew on the 2007 Baylor Religious Survey and Interview project to determine the extent to which people believe: (1) God loves the world, (2) God judges the world, and (3) God engages the world.[2]

As a result of their findings, they suggest that the American public can be split into four theological camps in terms of their belief about the nature of God:

1. Authoritative God—is both engaged and judgmental.
   Example: When Hurricane Katrina struck New Orleans, it was seen by many as the wrath of God against an area known for gambling, sin, and wickedness.
2. Benevolent God—is engaged yet nonjudgmental.

Example: Rudolph Giuliani wondered why God did not answer his prayers for healing when he was diagnosed with prostate cancer, which forced him to drop out of his Senate race against Hillary Clinton. Later a friend said that if Giuliani had not had prostate cancer and had remained in the race, he wouldn't have been mayor on 9/11 when he offered the calm and courageous leadership the nation needed.

3. Critical God—is judgmental but disengaged.

Example: During a visit to Brazil in 2007, Pope Benedict XVI delivered a speech to 6,000 people at a drug rehabilitation center in rural Guaratingueta. The pope warned that if the drug dealers didn't change their ways, they would face a future accounting of their life. Not necessarily in this life, but in the life to come.

4. Distant God—is nonjudgmental and disengaged.

Example: Benjamin Franklin once offered the following reflection on God: "I imagine it a great Vanity in me to suppose, that the Supremely Perfect does in the least regard such an inconsiderable Nothing as Man. More especially, since it is impossible for me to have any positive clear idea of that which is infinite and incomprehensible, I cannot conceive otherwise than that he the infinite Father expects or requires no Worship or Praise from us, but that he is even infinitely above it."[3]

Which is most popular? According to the study:

1. 31 percent believe in an Authoritative God
2. 24 percent believe in a Benevolent God
3. 24 percent believe in a Distant God
4. 16 percent believe in a Critical God
5. 5 percent are atheists

The authors are right to highlight the importance of this study. "A person's God is a direct reflection of his level of moral absolutism, his view of science, his understanding of economic justice, his concept of evil, and how he thinks we should respond to it."[4] But the significance of the study is not found only in the variant views of God in our culture; it is also the fluid nature of our thinking about

God as an ever-changing dynamic without any depth or mooring. As sociologist Rodney Stark reminds us, humans tend to adapt their images of God according to what best suits their immediate needs and life experience.[5]

Intriguingly, of those embracing the view of an authoritative God, 22 percent went to church several times a week as a child. This was true of only 16 percent of those embracing a benevolent view, 8 percent of those holding a critical view, 5 percent of those who believe God is distant, and 4 percent of atheists.

This suggests that the authoritative view of God, while active among the churched, is far from the dominant view among the unchurched. There you find the benevolent, critical, or distant views of God in full play. In my own experience, the more someone is unchurched, the more the scale slides from authoritative to benevolent, benevolent to critical, critical to distant, and finally, from distant to someone who has embraced an atheistic worldview.

So what is this God like? What does it mean for God to be distant, nonjudgmental, and not engaged? For that we need look no further than one of America's great unofficial spiritual leaders.

Her name is Oprah.

The Church of Oprah-Wan Kenobi

There can be little doubt about the power, influence, and inspiration of Oprah.[6]

Her career began at a local radio station when she was just nineteen years old. Then through hard work and talent she climbed her way up through the television ranks as newscaster and anchor, in Tennessee and Maryland, until finally, in 1984, she moved to WLS-TV in Chicago to host a local talk show, which became such a hit it eventually went national.

And the rest, as they say, is history.

Now she is arguably the best-known woman in the world, with an influence that extends into television, magazines, movies, book publishing, and the internet. By her twentieth anniversary as host of the *Oprah Winfrey Show*, she had become a billionaire and had assembled a US television audience of more than 49 million viewers each week—which does not include her broadcasts in 122 other countries. In 2010 *Forbes* magazine named her the most influential celebrity. Her latest venture? Her own television network.

But Oprah is more than a celebrity. She is even more than a brand or a business. She has become a shaping cultural force.

Oprah can single-handedly turn a book into a bestseller. On the other hand, she has been sued for crippling an entire industry simply by publicly denouncing its product. She even launches words; the *Wall Street Journal* coined the word *Oprahfication* to describe "public confession as a form of therapy." *Jet* magazine uses *Oprah* as a verb, with sentences like, "I didn't want to tell her, but . . . she Oprah'd it out of me." Even our political process has been altered, as politicians now hold "Oprah-style" town meetings.

But her most significant role may be that of America's spiritual guide. Much of her guidance is deeply Christian and highly commendable, pulling from her Baptist upbringing. In her book, *The Gospel According to Oprah*, Marcia Nelson outlines some of the orthodox and laudable aspects of Oprah's spirituality, including the themes of forgiveness, generosity, self-examination, gratitude, and community.

But there's more to her spirituality than a few broad, generic Christian themes. It increasingly reflects currents of thought embodied by such authors as Deepak Chopra, Marianne Williamson, and most recently, Eckhart Tolle. Nearly 5 million of Tolle's book *A New Earth* have been shipped with the Oprah seal on the front thanks to a series of ten live, Monday-night Web seminars featuring Tolle and Winfrey on Oprah's website. So popular were the webcasts that the first night brought down the server when more than 500,000 people tried to log on, and now millions have downloaded or streamed the first class.

So what are people learning?[7]

As Tolle writes in the foreword to his book *Stillness Speaks*, his thinking "can be seen as a revival for the present age of the oldest form of recorded spiritual teaching: the sutras of ancient India." Translation? Hinduism. Or as he packages it, an eclectic gathering of gleanings from Hinduism, Buddhism, and watered-down Christianity. Result? A fresh presentation of what was once called the New Age Movement, which tends to have four basic ideas:

1. *All is one, and one is all.* This means, of course, that "God is all, and all is God." Which also means that "I am God." In his book *The Power of Now,* Tolle writes that he doesn't like to use the word *God* or talk about finding God because it implies an entity other than you or me.

2. *Since most people don't realize they are God, they need to be enlightened.* This enlightenment can flow from many sources, including "spirit-channeling." Marianne Williamson, a frequent guest of Oprah's, garnered her first bestseller, *A Return to Love,* by popularizing "A Course in Miracles," which the author claims was dictated by a spirit voice that she says was Jesus, but not Jesus of Nazareth.

3. *Everything is relative.* What Tolle advocates, and what has been advocated by many of Oprah's guests, is that the truth is simply within you. Tolle writes, "The Truth is inseparable from who you are. . . . You are the truth." In fact, he distorts Jesus's famous statement, "I am the way, the truth and the life," by claiming that what Jesus meant was that he was his *own* truth, just as *we* can be *our* own truth.[8]

4. *Reincarnation—after death, the consciousness will reincarnate in another form.* Toward the end of *A New Earth,* Tolle writes, "When the lion tears apart the body of the zebra, the consciousness that incarnated into the zebra-form detaches itself from the dissolving form and for a brief moment awakens to its essential immortal nature as consciousness; and then immediately falls back into sleep and reincarnates into another form."[9]

This worldview is far from unique to Oprah. *Star Wars,* one of the most celebrated film series in history, was wrapped around many of those very same New Age ideas. So perhaps we shouldn't be surprised that a census in the Czech Republic found that over 15,000 citizens listed their religion as "Knights of the Jedi." They're not alone; New Zealand and Great Britain had already listed the "Jedi Church" among the formal religion options. Indeed in 2001 alone, over 390,000 Britons said that they practiced the religion. As the Church of the Jedi says on its website, Star Wars helped create the religion's terminology, but it did not create the faith itself.[10]

The intangible energy of the "Force" is, of course, a very appealing view of God. It is a god based on autonomous individualism.

To be autonomous is to be independent. The value of autonomous individualism maintains that each person is independent in terms of destiny and accountability. Ultimate moral authority is *self*-generated. In the end, we answer to no one but ourselves, for we are truly on our own. Our choices are solely ours, determined by our personal pleasure, not by any higher moral authority.

It reminds me of something a professor at one of the Claremont colleges in California said to me about autonomy's central place in the minds of people around the world. He quipped that it has produced a new argument against the existence of God: "It is a two-step proof," he suggests. "One, I am not living in a way that would honor a god, were he to exist. Two, therefore he does not exist."

Of course there is nothing new about New Age thinking. It dates back further than Hinduism. Indeed, it can be found in the opening chapters of Genesis, for it was the heart of the serpent's temptation of Adam and Eve (Gen. 3:1–5).

He challenged the idea of there being right or wrong: "*Now did God really say that you shouldn't do that?*"

He said that death is an illusion: "*You will not surely die.*"

He said that they could become divine: "*You will be like God.*"

He said that the way they would become like God is through enlightenment: "*You will know good from evil.*"

This is the unofficial folk religion of America in the early twenty-first century. We have eaten the forbidden fruit, only this time it didn't come in the form of an apple.

It came on a screen.

4

Unfortunate Godmongering

> Man is the being whose project is to be God.
>
> Jean-Paul Sartre[1]

When Stephen Hawking, who has been called the most revered scientist since Einstein, published his book *The Grand Design*, it quickly became the number one book on Amazon.

Not because it was a particularly well-written book—it wasn't.

Not because it contained any breakthroughs in physics or mathematics—it didn't.

No, it was because Mr. Hawking decided to officially announce that God is pretty much dead. "I regard the brain as a computer which will stop working when its components fail," he said in an accompanying interview with the *Guardian.* "There is no heaven or afterlife for broken down computers; that is a fairy story for people afraid of the dark."[2]

Hawking ended his bestselling *A Brief History of Time* in 1988 by suggesting that the discovery of a unified theory of physics could help us "know the mind of God."[3] As the *New York Times* noted, it

37

"was a line that—cynically, some thought—allowed glints of fuzzy sunshine to warm the cold blade of his thinking."[4]

The sun didn't stay out very long.

In our day it is the field of science and the writings of what some have called the "New Atheists," in which the divide between a Christian mind and a secular mind become most profound. As Harry Blamires writes, "To think secularly is to think within a frame of reference bounded by the limits of our life on earth: it is to keep one's calculations rooted in this-worldly criteria. To think Christianly is to accept all things with the mind as related, directly or indirectly, to man's eternal destiny as the redeemed and chosen child of God."[5]

In *The Grand Design*, Hawking maintains that the creation of our universe (and any others) "does not require the intervention of some supernatural being or god."[6] This is not a new position for Mr. Hawking—his former wife outed him as an atheist a few years ago.[7] And this is not the first time that Mr. Hawking has dabbled in what science writer Timothy Ferris calls "Godmongering." Nor is he the first scientist to use such sensationalism to sell books. Paul Davies may be the most shameless, with titles such as *God and the New Physics* and *The Mind of God*.

No Place for God

In 1984 the National Academy of Sciences, the nation's most eminent scientific organization, produced a book on the evidence supporting the theory of evolution (and arguing against the introduction of creationism or other religious alternatives in public school science classes). It published another in 1999. It has since produced a third, but with a twist, for it is intended specifically for the lay public. Further, it devotes a great deal of space to an explanation of the differences between science and religion, maintaining that the acceptance of evolution does not require abandoning belief in God.

Barbara A. Schaal, who is a vice president of the academy, an evolutionary biologist at Washington University, and a member of the panel that produced the book, said to the *New York Times*, "We wanted to produce a report that would be valuable and accessible to school board members and teachers and clergy."[8] Titled "Science, Evolution and Creationism," the seventy-page work asserts that "attempts to pit science and religion against each other create controversy where none needs to exist."[9]

So far, so good. The Genesis narrative does not speak to *how* God created, only *that* God created. The Christian has nothing to fear from science because the God of the Bible is the God of creation. All true scientific discoveries simply illuminate the world God has made.

The Scientist Embraces Atheism

When Stephen Hawking published *A Brief History of Time* in 1988, he suggested that the discovery of a unified theory of physics could help us "know the mind of God."

A little over twenty years later, Hawking published *The Grand Design* in 2010, maintaining that the creation of our universe "does not require the intervention of some supernatural being or god."

The significance of such "unfortunate godmongering" among scientists is how eager they seem to be to establish themselves as pastors and priests in a new secular society—and how willing we seem to be to ordain them. More people will read Hawking's stance on religion than will read the works of any of the top one hundred evangelical authors combined.

Ironic, since Hawking—along with many of his colleagues—has no place for God. In fact, Blamires's discussion of a Christian mind is precisely how the majority of scientists do *not* think. In fact, it is against this very type of thinking that they protest most violently.

But this is not what is meant by the report's desire to diffuse the tension between science and religion. Faith is upheld by trivializing it, reducing it to the likes of a favorite color or preferred style of music. As the report phrases it, science and religion deal with two different kinds of human experience. There is the experience that can be validated as fact (science), and there is the experience that can only be embraced in faith (religion). So believe what you want about God—that is your prerogative—just don't treat it like you would a scientific reality.

Granted, modern science is based on empirical evidence and testable explanation, and one cannot put God in a test tube and determine his existence. But there is more at hand here than science doing its job and knowing its limitations in regard to matters of faith. It is about *limiting* what *religion* can say about *science*. The working idea is that we can maintain our religious faith and our scientific discoveries *not* by seeing both as operating in the realm of public truth—to be jointly engaged and interpreted accordingly—but by seeing them as separate categories altogether that should never be allowed to intertwine. If you wish to believe in God, fine; just don't posit that this God actually *exists* as Creator or that he can actually be called on to explain anything.

In a recent article titled "Science on Faith," sociologist Elaine Howard Ecklund notes the influence of "nonoverlapping magisteria" (NOMA). The idea of NOMA was made famous by the late evolutionary biologist Stephen Jay Gould. For Gould, science and religion were two completely separate ways of discovering truth. Commenting on Gould's influence, Ecklund writes that according to the principles of NOMA, "Religion . . . operates within the realms of purpose, meaning and values, while science operates within the realm of empirical facts—and the two should respect but never interfere with each other." In other words, continues Ecklund, "The proper relationship between science and religion is no relationship at all."[10]

This is a relatively new cultural dynamic. As Ian Barbour notes, when religion first met modern science in the seventeenth century, the encounter was a friendly one. "By the eighteenth century many scientists believed in a God who had designed the universe, but they no longer believed in a personal God actively involved in the world and human life. By the nineteenth century," Barbour concludes, ". . . scientists were hostile to religion."[11]

In many ways, this is the new scientific project—reductive naturalism. *Naturalism* is the idea that nature is all that is. *Reductive naturalism* is the value that all that can be known within nature is that which can be empirically verified. So a reductive naturalism contends that what is real is only that which can be seen, tasted, heard, smelled, or touched and then *verified*—meaning it can be replicated in a test tube. Knowledge is *reduced* to this level of knowing. If it cannot be examined in a tangible, scientific manner, it is not simply unknowable; it is meaningless.[12]

Now here it is important to note how two paths diverged in the woods. Modern science relies on the empirical approach—the systematic collection of data through observation and experimentation. The core principle underlying this approach is *methodological naturalism*, which stipulates that "scientific hypotheses are tested and explained solely by reference to natural causes and events." This is not the same as *philosophical naturalism*, which is "the idea that all of existence consists of natural causes and laws, period." Pure methodological naturalism by itself does not rule out the possibility of entities or causes outside of nature—read "God"—only that they will not be considered within the framework of scientific inquiry.[13]

But this is precisely the mistake made by large numbers of scientists posing as religious pundits. From Stephen Hawking to Richard Dawkins, the idea seems to be that the existence of God is a scientific question, which confuses methodology with philosophy and is terribly misleading.

Defining Reductive Naturalism

- Naturalism—the idea that nature is all that is
- Reductive Naturalism—the value that states that all that can be known within nature is that which can be empirically verified; what is real is that which can be seen, tasted, heard, smelled, or touched and then verified—meaning it can be replicated in a test tube

---

Philosophical naturalism holds that life is accidental. There is nothing beyond ourselves that will ever bring order, reason, or explanation. We must restrict what can be known to that which is immediately before us, to what is *given* or *factual*. This means what can be empirically, or scientifically, demonstrated. As astronomer Carl Sagan argued in his final work, the goal is to rid ourselves of a "demon-haunted" world, meaning anything that challenges the rule of science and technology as the ultimate arbiter of truth and reality, for there is no other truth or reality to embrace.[14] Or as David Lindberg and Ronald Numbers write, "Nothing has come to characterize modern science more than its rejection of appeals to God in explaining the workings of nature."[15]

So the National Academy of Sciences is happy for religion to exist, and it does not want anyone to see a conflict between science and religion. But do not think they mean that those with religious conviction can pursue science with a religious worldview on equal footing as those who engage it with a naturalistic perspective. No, science and religion are encouraged to coexist—as long as religion knows its place.

Which is no place at all.

Another Earth?

The aggressive naturalism inherent within the mindset of modern science was put on display in late 2011 with reports about a newly discovered planet that is similar to earth—meaning potentially ideal for life.

A mere 600 light years away, Kepler 22b (named after the telescope) lies—like earth—within the habitable zone of its solar system. This means it's not too far and not too close to the home star for life, allowing a balmy temperature of 72 degrees across its surface. This zone is often called the "Goldilocks zone" because it's not too hot, not too cold, but just right. *Just right* means that water, which is necessary for life, doesn't freeze or boil. The planet also circles a star similar to our own, at about the same distance away from the planet as our sun, and with a year of 290 days.

Planet-hunting pioneer Geoff Marcy of the University of California, Berkeley, said, "This is a phenomenal discovery in the course of human history." But buried deep within the story, and sometimes not revealed at all, is that it's too big. Way too big. It's 2.4 times wider than earth and covered with water, making it more like the planet Neptune.[16]

So why the almost breathless tone of reporting? Because of something called the *anthropic principle*, from the Greek word *anthropos*, which means "man" or "human." The idea behind the anthropic principle is that our world is uniquely suited to human beings and carbon-based life—the only form of life known to science.

Very uniquely suited.

Astrobiologists have determined that as many as twenty factors are needed for a life-sustaining planet, or at least one that can sustain complex life. These include factors related to such things as:

- within Galactic Habitable Zone
- orbiting main-sequence G2 dwarf star
- protected by gas giant planets
- within Circumstellar Habitable Zone
- correct mass
- orbited by large moon
- magnetic field
- plate tectonics
- oxygen-rich atmosphere
- ratio of liquid water to continents
- terrestrial planet
- moderate rate of rotation

It has been estimated that for all of the right conditions to come together at the same time and on the same planet would be—well, astronomical. Despite billions of suns and planets, conservative figures would be one times ten to the negative fifteenth, or one one-thousandth of one trillionth.

Written out, the odds look like this:

$$\frac{1}{1,000,000,000,000,000}$$

Simply put, there are so many wonderful details that if changed only slightly would make it impossible for us to exist. The anthropic principle compels anyone to consider that somehow, some way, the earth was intentionally created for that very purpose.[17]

In the world of science, however, this is precisely what cannot be entertained. So instead of the lead story being the uniqueness of earth, which it truly is, the lead was how we found something that shared a handful of the same dynamics, as if to show that all we see and experience on planet earth happened by chance.

A very philosophical stance.

A Bad Dream

In truth, many scientists are very poor philosophers—and even worse theologians. Taking Hawking's conjectures to heart on the matter of heaven is as sound as taking those of the first man to orbit the earth, Yuri Gagarin, who sarcastically commented that on reaching outer space he failed to see God.[18] Consider the weakness of Hawking's rash conclusion about there being no need for God. As Alan Guth, the V. F. Weisskopf Professor of Physics at the Massachusetts Institute of Technology, has written, if the creation of the universe can eventually be described as a quantum process, we would still be left with a deep and abiding mystery: Where did the laws of physics come from?[19]

Few have engaged the dynamics of belief in relation to science more than physicist and theologian John Polkinghorne. In Polkinghorne's view, science and religion are simply concerned with different aspects of reality and thus are expressed differently. Both are equally concerned with the discovery of truth. Those who say science is concerned with facts while religion is simply a matter of opinion make the mistake of assuming that scientific facts are not, themselves, interpreted. And to say that religion is simply "shutting your eyes and gritting your teeth in a foolish attempt to believe impossible things" is ridiculous. Science and religion are simply asking different questions about the nature of reality. Science asks *how* while religion usually asks *why*. With a joint search for truth, they are friends rather than foes.[20]

As Michael Wenham wrote in response to Hawking, the universe "is certainly discoverable by science," but that is very different than making science the final word on its meaning. Science doesn't govern the universe; instead "science is governed by the universe."[21] Borrowing from an article by Alicia Cohn on pop icons, our cultural malady is that we let scientists have the power to define the worth of things and ideas.[22] And we are the ones who have given them that power. As Wenham adds, "Openness to the theoretical possibility of there being eleven dimensions and fundamental particles 'as yet undiscovered' shows an intellectual humility strangely at odds with writing off the possibility of other dimensions of existence."[23]

Like heaven.

5

Pseudo-Orthodoxy

The object of opening the mind, as of opening the
mouth, is to shut it again on something solid.

G. K. Chesterton[1]

What do you do with a book that has a whirlwind, edge-of-your-seat
opening—the creation of the heavens and the earth, followed by the
first humans, a talking serpent, history's first murder, a cataclysmic
flood—but then gets bogged down in seemingly endless pages of
begetting and smiting, Israelites versus Amalekites, and lots of old
men in beards? Sure, it picks up a bit with Potiphar's cougar wife, a
king's adultery after a pornographic bathing scene, and then Samson,
the first superhero. But after the sex of Song of Songs, what's left?
At least until the main character of the story—Jesus—arrives on the
scene. God in human form is a good read, no doubt, but you have to
go through thirty-nine of the sixty-six books to even get to that point.

What we need is a distillation of the canon that can be read in short
order, or so suspected a publisher from Canterbury, England, who
produced the *100-Minute Bible*. Launched at the famed Canterbury
Cathedral, the pocket-size, fifty-eight-page edition is for those who
don't have time to read the original, but are nonetheless interested in

the origins and message of Christianity. Audience? *The hurried and harried*. Far from a translation, even the word *paraphrase* would be, at best, loosely applied. The goal was to take the Bible and boil it down to the essentials. So after outlining the Ten Commandments, the *100-Minute* version adds: "Other more detailed laws governed diet, dress, personal relations, worship and every aspect of daily life."[2]

So much for Leviticus.

The intent of such efforts to offer a gateway to the Bible can certainly be understood. Biblical reading, not to mention biblical literacy, is in a free-fall. Efforts to make the Bible more accessible through modern translations (e.g., the New International Version, the New Living Translation, and the English Standard Version) along with helpful paraphrases (such as Eugene Peterson's *The Message*) not only serve but can be strategic. And the *100-Minute Bible* is far from the only innovation attempting to bring the Scriptures to an attention-challenged and biblically illiterate generation in new and arresting ways. The *Light Speed Bible* has been launched by Holman Bible Publishers with instruction on how to make it from cover to cover in as little as 16 to 18 hours. Zondervan has released both *The Bible in 90 Days* and *The Story*—a Bible written in novel-style format. Among Thomas Nelson's top sellers are *Biblezines*—magazine-style copies of the New Testament targeting specific consumers.

Not to be outdone, an Australian group has translated the entire Bible into SMS format, enabling verses to be sent direct to mobile phones. John 3:16 is now "God luvd da ppl of dis wrld so much dat he gave his only Son," and Genesis 1:1 "In da Bginnin God cre8d da heavens & da earth." The Bible Society in Australia, which translated all 31,373 verses of the Bible into text, claim they have remained 100 percent faithful to the original, building off of the Contemporary English Version and remaining faithful to the grammar (changing only the spelling of the words).

But when the essence of the Sermon on the Mount is reduced to "He taught that true happiness comes from having the right attitudes," as it is in the 100-minute version, something less than an outreach tool is at hand. As one reporter commented, this "could have come from the pen of a tabloid lifestyle columnist." And some of the greatest moments are seriously downplayed. "David achieved a wider fame when he overcame the giant Goliath" is akin to saying Michael Jordan became a better-known basketball player after winning his first slam-dunk contest. The author confessed that he "sacrificed poetry to clarity," but is that all that was sacrificed?[3]

Hardly. The reduction of content leads to the diminution of content. But that is precisely what plagues the mind of the culture at large.

Moralistic Therapeutic Deism

The National Study of Youth and Religion, conducted from 2001 to 2005 and perhaps the largest research project on the religious and spiritual lives of American adolescents, cataloged the demise of a Christian worldview *among Christians.*[4] While the vast majority of US teenagers identified themselves as Christian, the "language, and therefore experience, of Trinity, holiness, sin, grace, justification, sanctification, church, Eucharist, and heaven and hell appear, among most Christian teenagers in the United States at the very least, to be supplanted by the language of happiness, niceness, and an earned heavenly reward."[5]

Principal investigator Christian Smith writes, "It is not so much that U.S. Christianity is being secularized. Rather more subtly, Christianity is either degenerating into a pathetic version of itself or, more significantly, Christianity is actively being colonized and displaced by a quite different religious faith."[6]

Smith and his colleagues call this new faith "Moralistic Therapeutic Deism," a belief system that embraces the existence of a god who demands little more than to be *nice*, with the central goal of life to be happy and feel good about oneself. God is not particularly needed in daily life except to resolve various problems that may come our way (think Divine Butler or Cosmic Therapist). And regardless of religious convictions, beliefs, or commitments, good people go to heaven when they die.[7] What this results in is the widespread acceptance of relativism. Moral values become a matter of personal opinion or private judgment rather than something grounded in objective truth. This has become so entrenched that Allan Bloom, reflecting on his role as a university educator, maintained that there "is one thing a professor can be absolutely certain of. Almost every student entering the university believes, or says he believes, that truth is relative."[8]

When historian Mark Noll wrote that the scandal of the evangelical mind is that there is not much of an evangelical mind, his lament was largely that the mind possessed by Christians was not being applied.[9] The research of Smith reveals a more frightening scenario—the loss of the most basic content of Christian thought and belief itself.

Main Findings of the National Study of Youth and Religion

- Religion is a significant presence in the lives of many US teens.
- The character of teenage religiosity in the US is extraordinarily conventional.
- Very few US youth appear to be exposed to, interested in, or actively pursuing "spiritual but not religious" personal quests.
- The religiodemographic diversity represented by US adolescents is no more varied today than it has been for a very long time.
- The single most important social influence on the religious and spiritual lives of adolescents is their parents.
- The greater the supply of religiously grounded relationships, activities, programs, opportunities, and challenges available to teenagers, the more likely they will be religiously engaged and invested.
- At the level of subjective consciousness, adolescent religious and spiritual understanding and concern seem to be generally very weak.
- What we are calling Moralistic Therapeutic Deism appears to have established a significant foothold among very many contemporary US teenagers.

Source: National Study of Youth and Religion, 2008[10]

So what has influenced these young people toward such an emptying of content in regard to their faith? Alarmingly, three out of four students say that their beliefs simply mirror those of their parents.

This loss of content brings to mind Jean Bethke Elshtain's experience on the first Sunday following the attacks of 9/11. She went to a Methodist church in Nashville. The minister, whom she describes as having a kind of frozen smile on his face, said, "I know it has been a terrible week." Then, after a pause, he continued, "But that's no reason for us to give up our personal dreams." She thought, *Good grief! Shouldn't you say something about what happened and how Christians are to think about it?* But then she realized that if one has lost the term *evil* from his or her theological vocabulary, then it is not easy to talk about such a thing.[11]

But a robust and deeply theological discourse on evil was precisely what the world needed to hear at that moment and would have been uniquely served in hearing. Millions flooded to churches across the nation to hear a word from God, or at least about God, to make sense of the tragedy. Sadly, many were left as empty and lost as before they entered—which is one reason why the millions who came just as quickly left.

Little wonder that now even hell itself is in the dock, with popular pastors asking such questions as, "Is there a hell?" "Does anyone really go there?" and "Do your decisions in this life make or break you in regard to heaven and hell?" This is, of course, simply a reflection of culture. A study by the Pew Forum on Religion and Public Life shows that while 74 percent of all Americans say they believe in heaven, only 54 percent believe in hell.

In a day when the world is increasingly secular, and frequently apathetic, the Christian faith is losing its distinctive identity and content. And it is Christians who are emptying their minds. Yet without a clear embrace of the actual *matter* of the Christian faith, we will have nothing to offer the world that it does not already have.

This brings us back to the Bible as the primary source for the content of our faith. The Christian faith is not simply a defined worldview; it is a faith that claims to be based on *revelation*. Unlike a political system or body of humanly produced legislation, the Christian faith contends that God has chosen to reveal himself and truth about himself—through Scripture and supremely in Christ—that could not otherwise be known. The very meaning of the word *revelation*, from the Latin *revelatio*, is to "draw back the curtain," to reveal to us that which would have remained hidden had God not chosen to engage in the act of revelation.

The dilemma is that we are increasingly suspect of even the 100 minutes of this revelation that we read.

The Sermon on the Mount

(from *The 100-Minute Bible*)

Much of Jesus' teaching was brought together when, seated on a hillside, he spoke to his disciples about life in the kingdom of God. He taught that true happiness comes from having the right attitudes. Those who are humble, concerned about the world's sinfulness, gentle, devoted to goodness, merciful, single-minded in God's service, and peace-lovers will be blessed by God. Those of his followers who are persecuted in this world should rejoice, because they will have a rich reward in the next.

Jesus emphasised that he had not come to destroy the moral demands of the Jewish Law but to fulfil them. He taught that it is not enough not to commit murder; the anger which can lead to murder must be set aside too. It is not enough not to commit adultery; lustful thoughts must be set aside too. It is not enough to keep only our solemn promises; we should always mean what we say.

The Jewish Law taught that retaliation should be proportionate to the harm done—an eye for an eye and a tooth for a tooth—but Jesus taught that we should love our enemies and that we should return good for evil, turning the other cheek when others attack us.

He went on to say that ostentatious piety and charitable giving are wrong; both piety and giving should be between ourselves and God. No-one can serve two masters; it is impossible to serve both God and money. God knows what people's needs are and will supply them, in the same way as he provides food for birds and glorious clothing for flowers; we should not be anxious but should trust him. We should not judge others; for we shall be judged to the degree we judge. It is difficult to find the way to the kingdom of heaven and there will be those who will try to mislead us. We should assess others by the moral and spiritual quality of their lives.

He summarised the whole moral teaching of the Old Testament in the command to treat others as you would like them to treat you.

Jesus said that anyone who acts on his words is like a wise man who built his house on a rock. When storms came the house stood firm. But anyone who does not act on his words is like a man who built his house on sand. When storms came the house fell, and the ensuing devastation was great.

Matthew 5–7

Source: http://www.the100-minutepress.com/sample.htm

Taking It Literally

According to a recent article by Miguel De La Torre, a professor at Iliff School of Theology, "No one reads or interprets the Bible literally—regardless as to what they profess. To do so is simplistic, if not dangerous. All of us read our bias, our theology, and our social location into the text. There is no such thing as an objective reading; all readings are subjective."[12]

Welcome to hermeneutical nihilism.

But wait; it gets worse.

If we were to take it literally, we would then be forced to "live illegal—if not immoral lives." To prove his point, the learned professor prepared his own pop quiz:[13]

1. The biblical definition of a traditional marriage is one between a man and: (a) many wives or concubines, (b) sex slaves, (c) prostitutes, (d) his harem, (e) all of the above.
2. Homosexuals are to be: (a) tolerated, (b) encouraged, (c) killed, (d) banned.
3. Women are saved: (a) through baptism, (b) by reciting a sinner's prayer, (c) through child-bearing, (d) by accepting Jesus, who died for their sins, as Lord and Savior.
4. God tries to kill Moses, but does not because God is appeased by Moses's wife Zipporah, who: (a) cuts off the foreskin of her son's penis and rubs it on Moses's penis, (b) offers up a bull as sacrifice, (c) takes a vow of silence, (d) prays for forgiveness.
5. Evil and evil spirits come from: (a) God, (b) Satan, (c) neither *a* nor *b*, (d) both *a* and *b*.
6. Every year, one must take a tithe of all the land has yielded and: (a) give it to the priests, (b) give it to the church, (c) give it to the poor, (d) convert it to cash to buy wine, strong drink, or anything else their heart desires.
7. The Bible makes provisions for offering a sacrifice to: (a) nature, (b) the demonic god named Azazel, (c) God, (d) *a* and *b*, (e) *b* and *c*.
8. My response to taking this test will be: (a) stick my fingers in my ears and loudly sing "na na na na na," (b) question [the author's] salvation again while again stating never to read such

commentary, (c) ignore these parts of the Bible so I can maintain my literalism, (d) read the text for what it says and struggle with it in the humility of knowing that a clear answer may not be evident in this lifetime.

His list of answers?

1. e—1 Kings 11:3; Deut. 21:10–14; Gen. 38:15; Lev. 18:18
2. c—Lev. 20:13
3. c—1 Tim. 2:14–15
4. a—Exod. 4:24–26
5. d—1 Sam. 18:10; 1 Kings 14:10; Amos 3:6; Isa. 45:7
6. d—Deut. 14:22–27
7. e—Lev. 16:8, 10, 26
8. the choice is yours

I could teach an introductory course on how *not* to interpret *anything* based on this quiz. But it serves to illustrate the prevailing view that the Bible is dubious as any kind of truth source. The approach is devilishly disingenuous: simply associate taking the Bible literally with a ridiculously wooden interpretation of the Bible that violates the most fundamental rules of textual interpretation.

In truth, taking the Bible literally simply means that you take it at face value, which is the proper task of hermeneutics. If it is poetry, read and interpret it as poetry. If it is history, read and interpret it as history. It also means that you take into account the historical-cultural context as well as the wider theological context of the entire canon.

Is this so difficult to understand?

Apparently, the answer is *yes*, which is why a pseudo-orthodoxy permeates the church. The idea of orthodoxy is built off of its two root words: *ortho*, which means "right," and *doxos*, which means "thinking" or "belief." So the idea of orthodoxy is simply "right thinking"—and in relation to the Christian faith, right thinking in relation to revelation.

But if you only have 100 minutes of the Bible, and what you read can't be taken at face value, you're left with something less than orthodoxy.

You're left with something very much like moralistic therapeutic deism—which is very different than Christianity.

MINDSET

6

The Divine Supermarket

Man is quite insane . . . he creates gods by the dozens.

Montaigne[1]

A Jewish rabbi and Catholic monsignor decided to write a book that suggested searching for God has become like climbing a mountain. Since everyone knows that there is not just *one* way to climb a mountain—mountains are simply too big for that—there are any number of paths that can be taken. So the rabbi and priest concluded that all of the ideas about God throughout the religions of the world are like different ways up the mountain, and all of the names of God in all of the world's religions all name the same God. The Dalai Lama, who wrote the foreword to the book, heartily agreed.[2]

Few currents have shaped the mindset of our modern world more than *pluralization*. The process of pluralization is where individuals are confronted with a staggering number of ideologies and faith options competing for their attention.[3] Sociologist Peter Berger speaks of the traditional role of religion as a "sacred canopy" covering contemporary culture. Religion, at least in terms of the idea of there being a God whom life and thought had to consider, blanketed all of society and culture. Today that canopy is gone, replaced instead by millions of small tents under which we can choose to dwell.[4]

But the process of pluralization means far more than a simple increase in the number of faith options. The sheer number of choices and competing ideologies suggest that no single perspective or religious persuasion has the inside track about the spiritual realm.[5] Theologian Langdon Gilkey is correct when he observes that "many religions have always existed"; what is unique is a "new consciousness" that "entails a feeling of rough parity, as well as diversity, among religions." By parity, Gilkey means "the presence of both truth and grace in other ways."[6] Harold O. J. Brown adds that such pluralism is actually "value pluralism," meaning that "all convictions about values are of equal validity, which says in effect that no convictions about values have any validity."[7] In other words, not only are there lots of faith options from which to choose, but the fact that there are so many from which to choose means they are all equally valid.

Pluralization

The process of pluralization is where individuals are confronted with a staggering number of ideologies and faith options competing for their attention. The sheer number of choices and competing ideologies suggest that no single perspective or religious persuasion has the inside track about the spiritual realm.

This has fostered a smorgasbord mentality in regard to the construction of personal beliefs. As a result, Malise Ruthven calls America the "divine supermarket." The technical term is *syncretism*, the mix-and-match mentality of pulling together different threads in various religions in order to create a personal religion that suits our individual taste. Christianity becomes one of many competing boutique worldviews, no better or worse than another, that have set up shop in society's spiritual shopping mall for people to sample as a matter of personal preference.[8]

No better or worse, that is, until recently.

What 9/11 Did to Religion

On the occasion of the tenth anniversary of 9/11, CNN reached out to religious leaders and scholars to pose a simple question: How did 9/11 change America's attitude toward religion? According to those asked, 9/11 changed America's attitude toward religion in four very profound ways.[9]

1. *A chosen nation became a humbled one.* The random, arbitrary nature of what happened on that day altered the American sense of invulnerability. Our sense of being the "chosen" people has changed. We are now simply one nation among other nations. As Matthew Schmalz, a religion professor at Holy Cross University, offered: "We had this sense of specialness and invulnerability that 9/11 shattered."

2. *The re-emergence of Christo-Americanism.* Many believe an increase in religious prejudice, most notably against Islam, has occurred since 9/11. This has fueled the rise of what some have called Christo-Americanism—a distorted form of Christianity that blends nationalism, conservative paranoia, and Christian rhetoric. Charles Kammer, a religion professor at Wooster College in Ohio, says, "A segment of the religious community in the United States has been at the forefront of an anti-Islamic crusade that has helped to generate a climate of hatred and distrust toward all Muslims."

But it was the final two that were most profound and, arguably, the most factual.

3. *Interfaith became cool.* Before 9/11, interfaith efforts were dismissed as feel-good affairs that rarely got the media's attention. Now, being an interfaith leader is hip. "A generation of students is saying that they want to be interfaith leaders," says Eboo Patel, who founded the Interfaith Youth Core in 2002, "just like previous generations said they wanted to be human rights activists or environmentalists."

4. *Atheists came out of the closet.* After 9/11, atheists got loud. Richard Dawkins, Sam Harris, and Christopher Hitchens each authored best-selling books proclaiming the world would be better off without belief in God. According to Daniel Dennett, a philosophy professor at Tufts University, "Criticism of all religion, not just fanatical cults, was no longer taboo after 9/11."

In many ways, these are one and the same change. And this is the real story of religion after 9/11 and the way pluralism has manifested itself.

It seems counterintuitive, but after the prayers and packed churches the weekend following the tragedy of 9/11, not to mention Billy Graham's touching words in the National Cathedral, we seemed to decide that it was best to leave religion off the agenda.

And specifically, Christianity.

Ten years later, when the 9/11 Memorial was dedicated, no formal prayers were offered and no clergy were even invited. There was an interfaith prayer vigil at the National Cathedral featuring the dean of the cathedral (supposedly representing the Christian faith), but the invited guests did not include a single representative of Christianity, much less of evangelical faith. On the slate were a rabbi, a Buddhist nun, an incarnate lama, a Hindu priest, the president of the Islamic Society of North America, and a Muslim musician.

"Four Ways 9/11 Changed America's Attitude toward Religion"

by John Blake, CNN

1. A chosen nation became a humbled one
2. The re-emergence of Christo-Americanism
3. Interfaith became cool
4. Atheists came out of the closet[10]

The reason for this growing exclusion is Christianity's exclusivity—increasingly scandalous because of the pluralistic milieu in which we find ourselves. This exclusivity is, of course, unavoidable with a Founder who claims to be the way, the truth, and the life. Truth is fine as long as it is *a* truth but not *the* truth. Praying is fine, and even praying to Jesus. Just don't proselytize that you can *only* pray to Jesus. Little wonder that when Gandhi, who titled one of his books *All Religions Are True*, was asked what was the greatest handicap Jesus had in India, he instantly replied: "Christianity."[11] He meant the orthodoxy, the creeds, the substance of the faith, because when there is substance, there are truth claims. The exclusivism that came with the teachings of Jesus was the primary stumbling block for his acceptance.

And it is.

Christianity used to be rejected by Enlightenment intellectuals because they thought its central beliefs had been disproven by science or philosophy. Today orthodox Christianity tends to be disqualified on the grounds that it argues for a truth that is unchanging and universal.[12] A particular faith used to be wrong on the basis of what one perceived to be truth; now a faith is wrong for claiming there *is* truth. As Allen Bloom wryly noted, "The true believer is the real danger."[13]

And I do mean *danger*.

God Haters

A Brooklyn College professor dropped his bid to become chairman of the department of sociology due to outrage over his description of religious people as "moral retards." The controversial remarks, brought to the surface through his bid for chairmanship, come from an essay he published in an online journal in which he argued that religious people are incapable of moral action and that in the heart of Christians in particular you find "self-righteousness, paranoia, and hatred." What was apparently an earlier version of the online essay added, "Christians claim that theirs is a faith based on love, but they'll just as soon kill you." He even suggested that Christians have a greater proclivity toward child molestation.

For a taste of his rhetoric, here is a sample paragraph from the essay:

> On a personal level, religiosity is merely annoying—like pop music or reality television. This immaturity represents a significant social problem, however, because religious adherents fail to recognize their limitations. So, in the name of their faith, these moral retards are running around pointing fingers and doing real harm to others. One only has to read the newspaper to see the results of their handiwork. They discriminate, exclude, and belittle. They make a virtue of closed-mindedness and virulent ignorance. They are an ugly, violent lot.[14]

Claiming he was the victim of a political attack, the professor expressed anger at the treatment he received from other members of his department, as well as the administration's "inadequate" defense of his academic freedom. The irony, of course, is how the professor seemed oblivious to the venom of his own words and the lack of academic freedom it portended for people of faith in his department if he became chairman. A Brooklyn senior, Eldad Yaron, said: "This person has control right now on the content of many classes every student will take. Just imagine how fair and balanced these classes will be. . . . For a man who says religious people are inherently violent and incapable of moral action, to actually hire, promote, or evaluate a religious professor in good faith would be an impossible thing to do."[15]

Such incidents, sadly, are far from rare. In the summer of 2008 a University of Central Florida student removed a communion wafer from Catholic Mass and took it home, holding it "hostage." He was apparently upset that there was state-sponsored university funding of campus religious groups. The Eucharist, of course, is one of the seven sacraments in the teaching of the Catholic Church and is considered the literal presence of Christ. Understandably, his action outraged many Catholics. The student soon returned the wafer in a Ziploc bag.

There the story might have ended had science blogger and University of Minnesota professor Paul (PZ) Myers not gotten involved. Myers was disgusted at all of the hoopla surrounding the "frackin cracker" and referred to all Christian believers as delusional and irrational. Actually and more pointedly, as "demented f**kwits." So on his widely read blog he asked if anyone could "score *me* some consecrated communion wafers?" In return, he promised "profound disrespect and heinous cracker abuse, all photographed and presented here on the Web."

Again, more justifiable Catholic outrage.

Here are his comments on the matter:

> I wasn't going to make any major investment of time, money, or effort in treating these dabs of unpleasantness as they deserve, because all they deserve is casual disposal. However, inspired by an old woodcut of Jews stabbing the host, I thought of simple, quick things to do: I pierced it [the Eucharist] with a rusty nail (I hope Jesus's tetanus shots

are up to date). And then I simply threw it in the trash, followed by the classic, decorative items of trash cans everywhere, old coffee-grounds and a banana peel. My apologies to those who hoped for more, but the worst I can do is show my unconcerned contempt.[16]

One of the marks of our day is an increasingly open hostility toward faith and those who adhere to it.

Here is how Christopher Hitchens describes such religion:

> Violent, irrational, intolerant, allied to racism and tribalism and bigotry, invested in ignorance and hostile to free inquiry, contemptuous of women and coercive toward children: organized religion ought to have a great deal on its conscience.[17]

He even goes so far as to suggest that if religion were done away with altogether, there would be an end to war, intellectual enlightenment would blossom, and, one would infer, there would be an end to rush hour traffic.

The final sentence on the final page of his book?

"It has become necessary to know the enemy, and to prepare to fight it."[18]

And make no mistake about his "enemy." It isn't spirituality in general—that is innocuous and, in truth, meaningless. It is spirituality with a focus. Spirituality with a theology. Spirituality with a God. If it has form, content, and sinew, then it is, indeed, the enemy.

7

Neomedieval

History, we know, is apt to repeat itself.

George Eliot[1]

One of the more important understandings about our current cultural context, at least in the West, is that while we are living in a post-Christian era, the rising tide of secularism is most evident among the three shaping forces of culture: the epicenters of media, education, and the judicial system. Though the number of people who consider themselves a "none" on religious identification surveys has doubled, and the number who classify themselves as "unchurched" has risen by 50 percent (from 24 percent in 1991 to 37 percent in 2011), this does not mean that these people are secular in the sense that many of the leaders of the epicenters of culture are secular.

They are actually quite spiritual.

But in a *medieval* sense. Or perhaps more accurately, a *neomedieval* sense. To gain insight into this dynamic of culture, it is necessary to remind ourselves of the original medieval period and the torrent of history that followed it that led to our own culture.

Medieval

The middle ages, almost a thousand years in length, was not a single unit. Historians tend to divide it up into three eras: (1) the early middle ages, from AD 400 to 1000; (2) the high middle ages, from 1000 to 1300; and (3) the late middle ages, from 1300 to 1500.[2]

It is the early middle ages that come closest to earning the nickname "dark ages." After the fall of Rome to the barbarian Alaric in AD 410, there was a loss of learning, a loss of cultural cohesion, and a loss of order. It was a world that mixed Christianity with paganism.

But make no mistake; it was a deeply spiritual world.

In fact, the supernatural was everywhere—in places and days, people and events, filling people's lives with images, symbols, and ritual. In places such as Ireland, the earth and all in it was considered sacred; gods and goddesses roamed the landscape; the world of magic was embraced; but there was no God who sat in heaven, and there was no knowledge of a Christ who had come to earth.

As the middle ages went forward, particularly by the time of the high middle ages, the medieval world had become a profoundly Christian world. This was because missionaries refounded Western civilization and essentially reconverted the West back to Christianity from paganism—what Thomas Cahill referred to in the title of his book *How the Irish Saved Civilization*.[3]

Renaissance

Then came the Renaissance. As the word itself means, the *Renaissance* was a *rebirth*, for it was seen as a return to the learning and knowledge reflected in ancient Greece and Rome.

From the Renaissance came the creation of what many call *humanism*. As the name implies, much of this was simply a celebration of the humanities and humanity itself. At first this was a Christian, or *sacred*, humanism. Humanism only became destructive when it was ripped from its Christian moorings and became a *secular* humanism—when it became *autonomous*, to use Francis Schaeffer's term, meaning divorced from the anchor of biblical revelation and a Christian worldview. Instead of studying humans in light of the

Creator, there was a return to Protagoras's idea that "man is the measure of all things."

This was a radical reversal of medieval understandings.

With humans as the measure of all things, as opposed to God, what kind of world would there be? Many claimed it was *enlightened*, and in fact it was the Enlightenment that sprang from the Renaissance.

Enlightenment

To properly understand the Enlightenment, it must be seen as more than an age—it must be understood as a *spirit*. Rather than turning to revelation, there was a turn to reason as the surest and best guide for humanity. The motto of Immanuel Kant, one of the most significant thinkers of the time, was, "Dare to use your own reason"—or simply, "Dare to know." The fundamental idea was that we could begin with ourselves and gain the means by which to judge all things. And not only that we could, but that we *should*. The issue was not about the Enlightenment's relationship to religion but rather about the Enlightenment *as* a religion. So much so that many historians refer to the Enlightenment as the *rise of modern paganism*.

The speed by which Enlightenment thinking took hold was breathtaking. By the end of the era the church had been marginalized, theology dethroned as the queen of the sciences, and the Christian worldview reduced to a fading memory. For the first time since the fourth century, the church once again faced persecution.

Post-Modernity?

But then something began to happen. Many believed the Enlightenment era would be the last, greatest summit humanity needed to ascend. Yet people began to slip down the side of the mountain, finding Enlightenment thinking hard to grip. At first it was called *postmodernism*. There was much talk about what that meant, because no one was really quite sure. What we did know was that there was a changing view of reality, a new definition of truth, and a renewed openness to the spiritual.

It wasn't very enlightenment-ish at all.

But calling it postmodern, which simply means that which comes after modernity, didn't seem quite right. It didn't capture what was going on. So perhaps an easier thesis was: we're returning to the middle ages.

The early middle ages, to be exact.

Just as the fall of Rome threw people into a medieval world with its accompanying spirituality the first time, the fall of modernity and the waning of Christianity leading to our post-Christian state are throwing us into it again. Some suggest it may even be part of a larger cycle.

Brief Overview of Historical Eras

Middle Ages

- Divided into the early (or dark) middle ages from AD 400 to 1000, high middle ages from 1000 to 1300, and late middle ages from 1300 to 1500
- Began as deeply spiritual, but a world that mixed Christianity with paganism
- By the time of the high middle ages it became a profoundly Christian world

Renaissance

- A rebirth of learning and knowledge and the creation of humanism— a celebration of the humanities and humanity itself
- Humans, as opposed to God, became the measure of all things

Enlightenment

- Reason became the surest and best guide for humanity
- Fundamental idea was that we could begin with ourselves and gain the means by which to judge all things
- By the end of the era the church was marginalized and a Christian worldview was fading fast

Post-Modernity/Neomedieval

- A changing view of reality, a new definition of truth, and a renewed openness to the spiritual

The founder of Harvard University's department of sociology, Pitirim Sorokin, notes that civilization tends to swing in one of two directions: toward the material or toward the spiritual. One is rational or scientific, the other is more theological and aesthetic.

The medieval world was a spiritual world. From the Enlightenment forward, people have lived in a rational, scientific world. Our current shift is clearly back toward the spiritual. It is as though we are rediscovering the validity of faith. Books narrating spiritual journeys are bestsellers; spiritual themes run throughout contemporary music; films and television increasingly explore religious ideas and settings. People are interested in spiritual things, they're asking spiritual questions, and they are beginning to see that many of their deepest needs are spiritual in nature.

Author Douglas Coupland, who was the first to begin exploring what was then becoming known as *postmodernity* and who coined the early term "Generation X," expresses it well:

> Here is my secret: I tell it to you with an openness of heart that I doubt I shall ever achieve again, so I pray that you are in a quiet room as you hear these words. My secret is that I need God—that I am sick and can no longer make it alone. I need God to help me give, because I no longer seem to be capable of giving; to help me be kind, as I no longer seem capable of kindness; to help me love, as I seem beyond being able to love.[4]

But if we are entering a new era that is similar to the earlier medieval era, what does that mean? If we follow the medieval pattern, and I believe that in many ways we are, there will be at least five dynamics:

1. widespread spiritual illiteracy
2. indiscriminate spiritual openness
3. a deep need for visual communication
4. an attraction to spiritual experience
5. a widespread ethos of amorality

These dynamics, regardless of label, are clearly manifesting themselves. That is why the term *neomedieval*, first offered by Umberto Eco in regard to Western society, seems appropriate.[5]

This is why a medieval approach may need to be reimagined.

Patrick

When the great Christian missionary Patrick (ca. fifth century) entered the early medieval world, he had to engage the pagan elements.[6] He is said to have confronted and overpowered the druids and openly challenged a king by lighting a fire for an Easter celebration in open opposition to the edict that only one fire was to burn in the land, and that for the pagan feast of Bealtaine.

Patrick had to look for ways to connect the message of Christ to a pagan, but supernaturalized, world. In doing so, he imaginatively put himself in the position of the Irish. Looking for what they held in common, Patrick made clear that he too embraced a world full of magic. The difference between Patrick's magic and the magic of the druids was that in Patrick's world, "all beings and events come from the hand of a good God."[7] When Patrick arrived, the Irish were still practicing human sacrifice; he made it clear that through Christ's supreme sacrifice, such offerings were no longer needed. Patrick took an entire culture's leanings toward the spiritual and led them to Christ.

Much of this was done through the reimagining of symbol.

The First Symbol

I had the good fortune of seeing the exhibit "Treasures of Heaven: Saints, Relics, and Devotion in Medieval Europe" at the British Museum in London. For medieval Christians, contact with relics of Christ and the saints provided a unique bridge between earth and heaven. The relics themselves were often ordinary objects—a bone, a fragment of clothing. But they held great spiritual value because of whose bone it might have been or to whom the clothing had belonged.[8]

I was able to "see" such things as wood from the True Cross, hair from the apostle John, milk from Mary's breast, and a thorn from the crown of thorns placed on Jesus's head. I say "see" because by the time of the Reformation, many shared Calvin's skepticism about relics in general: "How do we know that we are venerating the bone of a saint and not the bone of some thief, or of an ass, or of a dog, or of a horse? How do we know that we are venerating the ring and the comb of the Virgin Mary rather than the baubles of some harlot?"[9]

Yet many of the most precious relics were gathered early on by Helen, the mother of Constantine, from her trips to the Holy Land. For example, it was during one such trip in AD 326 that she discovered the True Cross.

Intriguingly, when such relics have been allowed to be examined in more recent years, many have been found to bear the mark of authenticity. Consider the famed Tooth of St. John the Baptist: a dentist confirmed that it was indeed that of a thirty-year-old man from that era who ate a coarse diet.

Treasures of Heaven: Saints, Relics, and Devotion in Medieval Europe
British Museum

- Three thorns thought to be from the Crown of Thorns
- Fragments of the True Cross
- The foot of St. Blaise
- The breast milk of the Virgin Mary
- The hair of St. John the Evangelist
- The Mandylion of Edessa (one of the earliest known likenesses of Jesus)

Source: http://www.britishmuseum.org/whats_on/exhibitions/
treasures_of_heaven/introduction.aspx

The relics themselves were stored in ornate containers called reliquaries, made by the most skilled goldsmiths from the finest materials available. These relics then served as a personal focus for prayer, and they also were presented with great ceremony in public rituals. The locations of these relics became the destination of vast numbers of pilgrims.

I was struck by what dominated early Christian life in terms of image and symbol. If I asked you for the central symbol of the Christian faith, you would understandably say, "the cross." And perhaps today it is.

It wasn't to the first and earliest Christians. The cross as a symbol came on to the scene later, blossoming during the medieval era, often as reliquaries holding bits of wood from the True Cross. Called "speaking" reliquaries, the idea was that if the reliquary was to hold the bone of a hand, it was best to make your reliquary in the shape of a hand; if it was the heart of a saint, it was best to house it in a reliquary the shape of a heart.

Fragments of the True Cross were put into small crucifixes to represent what the reliquary held. But early on, no one tried to put forward the cross itself as the symbol of the Christian faith.

And for good reason.

It would have been like putting forward the image of an electric chair or a hangman's noose to honor a martyr in our day. The cross was not a work of art, much less something hung around your neck. It was a symbol of death and torture. Yes, Jesus died on a cross, but that didn't elevate the cross to anything more than a dark reminder.

So what was the prominent Christian symbol? When you survey early Christian art, and specifically reliquaries and tombs, it is the name of Christ himself.

Or at least the first two letters.

Here is what dominated early Christian symbolism and art:

The X is actually the written form of the Greek letter *chi*, and the P is the Greek letter *rho*. Together, *chi-rho* was the first two letters of *Christ* in the Greek language. Often superimposed on each other, they became the symbol for *Christ* and, as a result, the Christian faith.

If the cross was involved at all, it was portrayed with the *chi-rho* situated prominently at the top, reflecting how the cross had been stripped of its associations with humiliation and instead had become a symbol of triumph. It was Christ's triumph over and through the cross, not the cross itself, that was the point.

This is the nature of neomedieval spirituality—less interested in the cross than in who hung on it and why. All while in desperate need of it, for with the neomedieval comes, as before, the neopagan.

8

The New American Dream

> Greed is a bottomless pit which exhausts the person
> in an endless effort to satisfy the need without ever
> reaching satisfaction.
>
> Erich Fromm[1]

Back in 2000, three sociologists wrote a book titled *Millennials Rising: The Next Great Generation*. The authors were optimistic about "Generation Y"—or the "millennial" generation (referring to those born since the early 1980s, generally between 1980 to 1994).[2]

This generation would be more positive in outlook, socially oriented, with a "can-do" spirit. No Gen X slackers here, much less the manifestation of a rebel phase such as baby boomers went through in the sixties. It was even projected that under millennial influence, music would become more melodic and singable, sitcoms more wholesome, culture more mannered, individualism more restrained, and—well, you get the picture. Welcome to the most heroic, wholesome generation since the GIs returned from World War II.

That was the prediction in 2000.

Fast forward a few years.

In a spate of recent surveys, the millennial generation is being charted for what it really is: materialistic, liberal, socially isolated, and perhaps more captured by individualism than any previous generation.

More wholesome? According to a 2006 Pew Research Center poll, 61 percent of incoming college freshmen embraced same-sex marriage, 78.4 percent believed abortion should be legal, and one out of every five had no religious affiliation or were atheist or agnostic.[3]

More socially conscious? According to a 2006 UCLA study of incoming college freshmen, 81 percent said getting rich was one of their most important life goals. The second most popular answer, at 51 percent, was being famous. Compare this to a 1967 study of college freshmen in which 85.8 percent said one of their most important life goals was to develop "a meaningful philosophy of life," while only 41.9 percent thought it essential to be "very well off financially."[4]

As for being *social*, an article in the *Chronicle of Higher Education* featured a summary of insights into the millennial generation as offered by Richard T. Sweeney of the New Jersey Institute of Technology, along with excerpts from a panel discussion of millennials from Nevada State College and the University of Nevada at Las Vegas. When asked how many close friends they have, panelists were hard-pressed to name more than two. When asked how they relate to those "close" friends, it was almost entirely through Facebook or text messaging.[5]

A Picture of the Millennial Generation

According to a 2006 study of incoming freshmen by the Higher Education Research Institute at UCLA:

- 61 percent embraced same-sex marriage
- 78.4 percent believed abortion should be legal
- 81 percent said getting rich was one of their most important life goals

---

And what of individualism? As a *USA Today* article insightfully noted, this is the generation that grew up "in the glow and glare of their parents' omnipresent cameras." They have never been anything but the center of the universe. And reality doesn't have to bite—at least not yet. They can pursue their individualism by "becoming celebrities in their own worlds by posting videos on YouTube."[6]

Little wonder that consumer psychologist Kit Yarrow of Golden Gate University in San Francisco fears a growing "sense of emptiness and depression" as millennials age. "They're putting their resources and energy and validation and self-worth into what people who aren't close to them think of them, which is fame."[7]

The New American Dream

But fame is just a stepping-stone. In an opinion piece for the *Boston Globe*, Neal Gabler suggests that the idea of the American Dream has changed dramatically in recent years.

As devised in the late nineteenth century, the American Dream was about *opportunity*. The idea, writes Gabler, "was that anyone in this pragmatic, un-class-conscious society of ours could, by dint of hard work, rise to the level of his aspiration."[8] Opportunity is very different than entitlement. As opposed to what is deserved, opportunity is the promise of a chance to have your choices, work, character, and resolve result in due reward. And in most cases, that due reward is not fame or fortune but the ability to earn a living, be sheltered, and provide for the needs of your family.

But over the last fifty or so years, the American Dream has changed. The dream is "no longer about seizing opportunity but about realizing perfection. . . . The career has to be perfect, the wife has to be perfect, the children have to be perfect, the home has to be perfect, the car has to be perfect, the social circle has to be perfect." And we will seemingly do whatever it takes to attain this perfection, from "plastic surgery to gated communities of McMansions to the professionalization of our children's activities like soccer and baseball to pricey preschools that prepare 4-year-olds for Harvard."[9]

Or else.

At least that's how we feel. Because inherent within the new American Dream is a new competition from those who are also striving for perfection and may have already attained it. People "whose wives will always be beautifully coiffed and dressed or whose husbands will be power brokers, whose children will score 2,400 on their SATs and who will be playing competitive-level tennis, whose careers will be skyrocketing, whose fortunes will be growing."[10]

So if you are not in on the perfection, you are not only left behind but you are second rate.

So, Gabler concludes, welcome to the new American Dream. Not where every little girl can have the opportunity to get an education and strive to reach her full potential, limited only by her hard work, persistence, and dedication. No, today it is the birthright of every girl "to be a rich, beautiful, brilliant, powerful, Ivy League-educated Mistress of the Universe who will live not just the good life but the perfect one."[11]

I think Gabler is on to something. Only he didn't go far enough. If the original American Dream was *opportunity* (the rags-to-riches Horatio Alger story) that then morphed into perfection, it has now become *entitlement*.

Entitlement is beyond perfection. Yes, perfection is our goal, but instead of the dream being striving for perfection—and achieving it—the newest American Dream seems to be the demand for it to come our way as an inalienable right. Regardless of whether we've earned it or not, it should be provided. It is our due.

What Is the Horatio Alger Story?

Horatio Alger (1832–1899) was the author of many adventure stories in which the central character was a boy who was born into adversity and poverty and then led an exemplary life to overcome the odds and find success.

It would be difficult to eavesdrop on our culture and not sense this shift—how the great American Dream has turned into the great American Right: "I am *entitled* to the perfect car, house, spouse, child, and job." So we do not expect a *chance* at a job but the *guarantee* of one. And not just any job, but the dream job that gives us everything we desire through fulfillment, meaning, and compensation.

Captive to Consumerism

Little wonder that in his third installment of his multiyear study of the next generation, sociologist Christian Smith found that eighteen- to twenty-three-year-olds are "captive to consumerism." Few were able to even fathom taking up the mantle of living modestly or simply. As Smith notes, the "vast majority of emerging adults . . . came out strongly in favor of a financially unconstrained, materially comfortable lifestyle spent by them and their families consuming a variety of rewarding goods, services, and experiences."[12] Smith posed a number of questions, all variants of "What makes a good life?" He purposefully did not focus or lead the questions toward consumerism or materialism. It's enlightening to let the answers speak for themselves:

> "Buying stuff really makes me happy."
>
> "If you've been successful and well enough off, I think that you should indulge yourself."
>
> "I want to earn, between me and my wife, at least a quarter of a million dollars a year. That's a number, I guess, I'd be satisfied with making that."
>
> "A good life for me would be to have more than enough money than I actually need, and live like a kid the rest of my life. . . . You only live once, and if you have the chance to live in excess, why not?"
>
> "If I could have $5 million . . . that's a good life."
>
> "Eventually, I want to live in a big house and have a really good car, that's why I'm going through college to get a job, so I can get these things."[13]

Narcissistic Hedonism

The name for this is *narcissism*. More specifically, *narcissistic hedonism*.

In Greek mythology, Narcissus is the character who, on catching a glimpse of his reflection in the water, becomes so enamored with himself that he devotes the rest of his life to his own reflection. From this we get our term *narcissism*—the preoccupation with self.

The value system of narcissistic hedonism is the classic "I, me, mine" mentality that places personal pleasure and fulfillment at the forefront of concerns. Or as Francis Schaeffer maintains throughout his writings, the ultimate ethic of our day is the pursuit of personal peace and individual affluence. In terms of how this new American Dream plays out spiritually, noted cultural historian Christopher Lasch christens ours "the culture of narcissism," determining that the current taste is for individual therapy instead of religion. The quest for personal well-being, health, and psychic security has replaced the older hunger for personal salvation.[14] It is as though we have settled for a redemption that salvages this world alone.

Philip Rieff writes that therapy has become "the unreligion of the age, and its master science." In a therapeutic understanding of the world there is "nothing at stake beyond a manipulatable sense of well-being." Roger Lundin suggests that a therapeutic culture brackets off questions of ultimate concern—about the nature of the good, the meaning of truth, and the existence of God—and focuses on the "management of experience and environment in the interest of that 'manipulatable sense of well-being.'"[15] And in so doing, it makes that sense of well-being *everything*. There is no view of heaven to lift our gaze beyond the pale of this world and no fear of hell to drive us to forsake it.

This runs deeper than mere self-gratification. Narcissism has become a guiding worldview. Stanley Grenz observes that Anselm's famed dictum, "I believe in order that I may understand," was altered by the Enlightenment to become, "I believe what I can understand."[16] The modern twist goes further, becoming, "I believe when I understand that it helps me."

Such consumer-driven pragmatism has been seen before. Many have wondered how Hitler could have advanced his horrific agenda through the German people, culminating in World War II and the Holocaust. While complex and multifaceted, a key dynamic was a promised utopia of personal peace and affluence. This then became the basis of what could be accepted as moral and true. Historian Michael Burleigh's assessment is that there was simply a moral collapse as people "chose to abdicate their individual critical faculties in favor of politics based on faith, hope, hatred and sentimental collective self-regard for their own race and nation."[17]

In the end, the Germans found that such preoccupation with self failed to deliver. As Daumier depicted Narcissus in a series of lithographs on the ancient Greek and Roman myths, the reflection that so captivated his life was not, in fact, an accurate portrait. Thin and gaunt, almost comical in face, H. R. Rookmaaker notes that he was a "starving idiot, grinning at his own hollow cheeks."[18]

Feasting on yourself is a very sparse meal.[19]

The names say it all: YouTube. MySpace. And, of course, the *I*'s— iPod, iTunes, iMac, iPhone, and iPad.

You, my, I.

If there is a theme to our day, it's that *it's all about me*. Tom Wolfe had earlier labeled the 1970s the "Me Decade." In her book *Generation Me*, Jean M. Twenge writes that compared to today's generation, "They were posers."[20]

9

Wikiworld

For to put the matter at its baldest,
We live in a thought-world,
And the thinking has gone very bad indeed.

Saul Bellow[1]

Among the internet's most popular sites is Wikipedia, the online encyclopedia, which is written entirely by unpaid volunteers. Though praised for democratizing knowledge by such luminaries as Stanford University law professor Lawrence Lessig, Wikipedia has had more than its fair share of detractors. The site drew unwanted attention when journalist John Seigenthaler exposed gross errors and fabrications in the entry on his life. Numerous scholars have voiced concern that the encyclopedia is an unreliable research tool and lament students' use of the resource. A paper by a University of California, Merced, graduate student revealed many of Wikipedia's flaws, including often-indifferent prose and some serious problems with accuracy.

Yet Wikipedia, it seems, is here to stay. The English-language version of the encyclopedia has nearly four million articles, and the site is consistently rated as one of the Web's ten most popular destinations.[2] There is even an annual international conference for the Wikimedia community—Wikimania.

Truthiness

Truthiness is sort of what you want to be true, as opposed to what the facts support. Truthiness is a truth larger than the facts that would comprise it—if you cared about facts, which you don't, if you care about truthiness.

Stephen Colbert

Regardless of how accurate certain articles may or may not be (and in fairness to Wikipedia, a study by the journal *Nature* found Wikipedia's articles on science nearly as accurate as those that appear in the *Encyclopaedia Britannica*), and separate from the movement advocating free access to information online, political satirist Stephen Colbert has put his finger on the real issue in his coining of a single term: *Wikiality*.

Colbert is the host of the *Colbert Report* on the Comedy Central television network (a satirical spin-off of the *Daily Show with Jon Stewart* and a purposeful spoof on Fox's Bill O'Reilly). Wikiality is "reality as determined by majority vote," such as when astronomers voted Pluto off their list of planets. Colbert notes that any user can log on and make a change to any entry, and if enough users agree, it becomes "true." If only the entire body of knowledge could work this way, offers Colbert. And through a new Wikiality, he maintains it can. "Together we can create a reality we can all agree on. The reality we just agreed on."[3]

Colbert debuted his show by introducing another cultural reflection: *truthiness*, which suggests that actual facts don't matter. What matters is how you feel, for you as an individual are the final arbiter of truth. In an interview Colbert said, "Truthiness is sort of what you want to be true, as opposed to what the facts support. Truthiness is a truth larger than the facts that would comprise it—if you cared about facts, which you don't, if you care about truthiness."[4]

So Wikiality allows you to take your truthiness and make it fact through majority vote. While obviously the substance of a comedy sketch, there is something profoundly substantive and telling here.

There have been three major theories of truth throughout the history of Western thought. The first, and most dominant, has been

---

Theories of Truth

- *Correspondence Theory*: there is a direct correlation between truth and reality; this provides the foundation for much of evangelical theology
- *Coherence Theory*: truth is that which hangs together as a system of thought in superior fashion to other systems of thought
- *Pragmatic Theory*: what is true is that which *works*
- *Democratization Theory*: truth is what the majority take it to be; there is no truth outside of what the majority determines

---

the *correspondence theory* of truth. The idea is simple: If I say, "It is raining," then either it is raining or it is not. You simply walk outside your door and discover whether my statement corresponds with reality. A second theory regarding the nature of truth is often called the *coherence theory*, which is the idea that truth is marked by coherence—meaning a set of ideas that do not contradict each other. A third major contender for the idea of truth is the *pragmatic theory* of truth. When someone is being pragmatic, he or she is pursuing a course of action because it achieves an end result. So a pragmatic theory of truth maintains that what is true is that which *works*.

Taking truthiness into the world of Wikiality allows a new theory of truth to insert itself into our psyche: truth is what the majority take it to be. So with the democratization of knowledge comes the *democratization of truth*, resulting in an evolution of the idea that "what is true for you is true for you, and what is true for me is true for me" to "what is true for us is true for us," but not necessarily its corollary, which would be "and what is true for them is true for them." In a world of Wikiality, there is no truth outside of what the majority determines. Fifty-one percent become the final arbiter of reality. Or as Marshall Poe wrote in the *Atlantic*, "Wikipedia suggests a different theory of truth. . . . If the community changes its mind and decides that two plus two equals five, then two plus two does equal five."[5]

A very truthy idea, to be sure, but not a very biblical one.

But it is the mark of our world.

Wikiworld

A *Wiki* is a document or process on the Web that anyone can add to
or modify. And most of us are now familiar with internet companies
where the sites' visitors create the content. Silicon Valley insiders call
it Web 2.0, signifying a second generation of internet. What we may
not realize is how this 2.0 generation may be looked back on as the
forerunners of a massive cultural change.

In his seminal book *The World Is Flat*, Thomas Friedman argues
that there have been three great eras of globalization. The first, what
Friedman calls Globalization 1.0, lasted from 1492—essentially from
when Columbus set sail, opening trade between the Old World and the
New World—until the start of the nineteenth century. This shrank the
world from a large size to a medium size, largely through countries
and muscles.

The second era, Globalization 2.0, lasted from 1800 to 2000. Though
interrupted by the Great Depression and two world wars, this era
shrank the world from a medium size to a small size. The driving
force of this era's global integration was multinational companies.

Friedman argues that around the year 2000 we entered the era of
Globalization 3.0, shrinking the world from a small size to a tiny size
and flattening the playing field at the same time. While Globalization
1.0 was about countries globalizing, and Globalization 2.0 was about
companies globalizing, Globalization 3.0 is about individuals globalizing. Not through horsepower or hardware, but through software.
"Individuals must, and can, now ask: Where do I fit into the global
competition and opportunity of the day," notes Friedman, "and how
can I, on my own, collaborate with others globally?"[6]

This new freedom is, indeed, new. As Don Tapscott and Anthony
Williams have noted, throughout history people tended to be subor-
dinate to something or someone. Now, profound changes in technology, demographics, and the global economy are giving rise to powerful
new models based on community, collaboration, and self-organization
as opposed to hierarchy and control. We live in an "open source"
world where "crowd wisdom" reigns supreme.[7] On the business level,
this is appealing. "Billions of connected individuals can now actively
participate in innovation, wealth creation, and social development in

ways we once only dreamed of," write Tapscott and Williams. "And when these masses of people collaborate they collectively can advance the arts, culture, science, education, government, and the economy in surprising but ultimately profitable ways."[8] The dilemma is that this transcends such things as Wikipedia or the Linux operating system. Beyond Wikinomics is something more substantive, and more telling: *Wikiworld*.

Three Great Eras of Globalization
Thomas Friedman, *The World Is Flat*

- *Globalization 1.0*: lasted from 1492 to the start of the nineteenth century, shrinking the world from a large to medium size through countries and muscles
- *Globalization 2.0*: lasted from 1800 to 2000, shrinking the world from a medium size to a small size through multinational companies
- *Globalization 3.0*: from 2000 to the present, shrinking the world from a small size to a tiny size, largely through the internet and software

---

And in a twisted irony, the collective becomes, in the end, individual. It may seem to be *we the people*, but it is really *me the individual*. The *power of us* is really the *supremacy of me. Unleashing our collective genius* becomes *asserting my personal opinion*. At one level, of course, this is being widely recognized. One need look no further than *Time* magazine in 2006 choosing *You* as person of the year, complete with a Mylar mirror on the cover for better self-reflection. In picking *You*, *Time* noted the shift from institutions to individuals who are "transforming the information age" through websites such as YouTube and Facebook.[9] But the transformation, and thus the significance of the transformation, may run much deeper than *Time*'s early nod.

The heart of the change involves the ever-widening rejection of professional and intellectual elites and the diminution of those organizations that either exist as the gathering of such elites or serve as the repositories of their supposedly exclusive knowledge. Translation: the loss of any sense of an external authority. That means a Wikiworld shaped by individuals who answer to no voice but their own.

Autonomous Individualism

A few years ago, I was listening to public radio and heard an interview with a juvenile court judge. He said that in his court, he had seen violent juvenile crimes triple over recent years. The reporter asked him why he thought that was happening. He replied, "First, kids lost the *admiration* of authority. Then, they lost *respect* for authority. Now, they've lost the *fear* of authority."

The displacement of authority's role in culture flows from an increasing autonomous individualism. To be *autonomous* is to be independent. The value system of *autonomous individualism* maintains that each person is independent in terms of destiny and accountability. Ultimate moral authority is *self*-generated. In the end, we answer to no one but ourselves, for we are truly on our own. Our choices are solely ours, determined by our personal pleasure and not by any higher moral authority. Intriguingly, Thomas Oden notes that this is the force behind the idea of heresy. The "key to *hairesis* (root word for *heresy*) is the notion of choice—choosing for *oneself*, over against the apostolic tradition."[10]

In reviewing the past five hundred years of Western cultural life, Jacques Barzun concludes that one of the great themes is *emancipation*, the desire for independence from all authority. Barzun concludes that for the modern era, it is perhaps the most characteristic cultural theme of all.[11]

In Wikiworld, there are "a billion personalized truths, each seemingly valid and worthwhile." As Andrew Keen, the founder of the world's largest privately owned public relations company, observed, "In this era of exploding media technologies there is no truth except the truth you create for yourself." The Silicon Valley entrepreneur calls it the "great seduction":

> The Web 2.0 revolution has peddled the promise of bringing more truth to more people—more depth of information, more global perspective, more unbiased opinion from dispassionate observers. But this is all a smokescreen . . . [the] chilling reality in this brave new digital epoch is the blurring, obfuscation, and even disappearance of truth.[12]

A New Babel

The great danger of autonomous individualism goes beyond something as seemingly benign as a Wikipedia entry. It was this same spirit of autonomous individualism that influenced those who erected the infamous tower of Babel, and it is leading to its rebuilding today. Only this time we are not building with bricks and mortar but with silicon chips and genetic engineering. We live in a technological age, and we have embraced technological advance with abandon, creating what Neil Postman terms a *technopoly*, where technology of every kind is cheerfully granted sovereignty.[13] Or, as Jacques Ellul writes, at least the *process* of technique designed to serve our ends.[14]

Ironically, within the word *technology* itself lies the new philosophical mooring that marks our intent. The word is built from such Greek words as *technites* (craftsman) and *techne* (art, skill, trade), which speak either to the idea of the person who shapes or molds something or to the task of shaping and molding itself. But it is the Greek word *logos*, to which *technites* is joined, that makes our term *technology* so provocative. In Greek thought, *logos* is a reference to divine reason, or the organizing principle of the world. In John's Gospel, *logos* is used to communicate to those familiar with the Greek worldview the idea of the divinity of Jesus. Moderns have put together two words that the ancients would not have dared to combine, for the joining of the words intimates that mere humans can shape the very order of the world. Though technology itself may be neutral in its enterprise, there can be no doubt that within the word itself are the seeds for the presumption that would seek to cast God from his throne and assert humanity in his place as the conduit of divine power.[15]

And we have wasted little time.

On July 25, 2003, the first test-tube baby turned twenty-five. Robert Edwards, who along with his partner, Patrick Steptoe, pioneered the procedure, graced the occasion with a rare but candid interview with the *Times* of London. "It was a fantastic achievement but it was about more than infertility," said Edwards, then seventy-seven and emeritus professor of human reproduction at Cambridge University. "I wanted to find out exactly who was in charge, whether it was God himself or whether it was scientists in the laboratory."

Smiling triumphantly at the reporter, he said, "It was us."[16]

10

Forgetting How to Blush

Sin is a queer thing. It isn't the breaking of divine commandments. It is the breaking of one's own integrity.

D. H. Lawrence[1]

If music provides a window into our world, or if music itself even influences and shapes culture—have you been listening to the radio lately? Or checked out the top iTunes downloads?

You should.

Here are the top songs from one week in 2011.[2] The titles speak for themselves in terms of their character and intent. For the ones that may not, I've explained the theme.

- "F**kin' Perfect" by Pink
- "Born This Way" by Lady Gaga
  For all intents and purposes an anthem for the lesbian, gay, bisexual, transgendered lifestyle.
- "F**k You" by Cee Lo Green
- "Tonight" by Enrique Iglesias
  Encourages promiscuity and includes adult language and content.

- "Hey Baby" by Pitbull
  Descriptively encourages promiscuity and includes the line, "Now let me see where the Lord split ya."
- "S & M" by Rihanna
  Yes, that S & M.

So let's add this up. Among the top songs, two have the f-word in the title, and four others promote—and I do mean *promote*—rampant promiscuity, including homosexuality and sadomasochism.

And no one seems to be concerned.

Whatever Happened to Sin?

In 1973 psychiatrist Karl Menninger published a book with the provocative title *Whatever Became of Sin?* His point was that sociology and psychology tend to avoid terms like *evil*, *immorality*, and *wrongdoing*. Menninger details how the theological notion of sin became the legal idea of crime and then slid further from its true meaning when it was relegated to the psychological category of sickness.[3]

Sin is now regarded as little more than a set of emotions that can be explained through genetics. So something like lust is not a wrong that threatens our own health and the well-being of others; it's simply an emotional urge that is rooted in the need to propagate the human species. It's fixed in our genes.

We've become so uncomfortable with acknowledging the idea of sin and evil, particularly in our own life, that we've even tried to turn it into a virtue: lust becomes sensuality, and anger just means being honest with your emotions.

An example of Menninger's thesis can be found in the news regarding major league baseball's highest-paid player, Yankees third baseman Alex Rodriguez, who admitted he took performance-enhancing drugs from 2001 to 2003. In an interview with ESPN's Peter Gammons, Rodriguez spoke candidly about why he took the drugs that are, of course, illegal. A-Rod said he felt pressured to take them, that the culture was loose, and that he was young and stupid. He even said he was sorry for doing it. So what was he guilty of? Being negligent, naïve, and not asking the right questions.

Anything but guilty of a sin.

When he was asked whether he had *lied* when in an earlier interview with Katie Couric he denied using steroids, human growth hormones, or other performance-enhancing substances, he replied, "At the time . . . I wasn't even being truthful with myself. How am I going to be truthful with Katie or CBS?"[4] It seems we are one of two types of people: *mistakers* or *sinners*. Our culture's verdict is clear:

We are *mistakers*.

And it's not just moving from sinner to mistaker; it's redefining what should be considered a sin to begin with.

According to the most comprehensive national survey of sexual behaviors released by the federal government, slightly more than half of all American teenagers (ages fifteen to nineteen) have engaged in oral sex, with males and females reporting similar levels of experience.[5]

Claire Brindis, professor of pediatrics at the University of California, San Francisco, observes that "at 50 percent, we're talking about a major social norm. It's a part of kids' lives."[6] The report, released by the National Center for Health Statistics in Hyattsville, Maryland, shows that the figure increases to about 70 percent of eighteen- to nineteen-year-olds. But the deeper cultural shift is not how many teens engage in oral sex, but how the majority of teens do not even consider oral sex to *be* sex.

Or think of how premarital intercourse is increasingly considered the norm and is glamorized through such programs as MTV's reality show *16 and Pregnant*.[7]

Words Dropped from the 2008 Edition of the *Oxford Junior Dictionary*

- abbey
- altar
- bishop
- chapel
- christen
- disciple
- monk
- saint
- sin

Moral Individualism

In his massive study of emerging adults, Christian Smith found that six out of ten (60 percent) interviewed expressed a highly individualistic approach to morality. In other words, morality is a personal choice that is "entirely a matter of individual decision. Moral rights and wrongs are essentially matters of individual opinion in their view."[8] Further, one in three said they simply don't know what makes anything right or wrong.

Here are the eighteen- to twenty-three-year-olds in their own words:

> "I have never heard anybody else that has anything like it [my moral outlook] and I just don't know where it came from. Like just kinda things that I thought up, that I decided was right for me."

> "What's a moral rule, though? A personal thing? Well then I would say that sometimes breaking a moral rule might be all right, depending on the situation."

> "Wrong are the things that change things for way worse than they were before—and I kinda think again it's totally relative to the person, it depends on where you wanna go and what you wanna do."

> "I don't think lying is wrong necessarily. It's life. People lie. That's my view on the whole thing. Everyone's done it. It's not going to go away."

> "I will do what I can to get ahead in this world while I'm here."

> "I would do what I thought made me happy or how I felt. Because I have no other way of knowing what to do but how I internally feel. That's where my decisions come from. From *me*. My decisions come from inside of me."[9]

So why not just do away with the word *morality* altogether? That's exactly what *is* happening. The latest edition of the *Oxford Junior Dictionary* for children made it official. In a sweeping revision, "crucial words used to describe . . . traditional topics have been stripped . . . in favour of more 'modern' terms." Among the entries that have vanished in the most recent edition: *abbey, altar, bishop, chapel, christen, disciple, monk, saint,* and, yes, *sin*.[10]

It brings to mind the words of the prophet Jeremiah to the people of his day: "Are they ashamed of their detestable conduct? No, they have no shame at all; they do not even know how to blush" (Jer. 6:15).

There could be no greater cultural indictment.

Or warning.

A Culture of Lies

What lies at the heart of a culture that no longer knows how to blush is a culture that no longer knows the truth. As the apostle Paul once observed of the decadent culture of his own day, "God gave them over in the sinful desires of their hearts to sexual impurity for the degrading of their bodies with one another." And why did this happen? Paul continues, "They exchanged the truth of God for a lie" (Rom. 1:24–25).

I once compiled a quick list, more to be provocative than exhaustive, of some of the day's leading lies. When I finished, I think I was most disturbed by how familiar they were to my ears, as if I had assembled a list of proverbs to which anyone would assent:

1. It doesn't matter what you believe as long as you are sincere, since all religions are basically the same (corollary: there are many ways to God).
2. Christians are anti-science/anti-intellectual, and anyone who is a Christian must have checked their brains at the door.
3. Marriage and family are purely social constructs and are therefore plastic and malleable by the current society.
4. Personal significance and importance lies in gaining fame and wealth. The person who dies with the most toys wins.
5. There are no absolute, transcendent truths in the moral or spiritual realm. All such truth is relative.
6. Sex is physical, not spiritual. Do with it as you will.
7. Science is the ultimate arbiter of truth and determinant for both fact and meaning.
8. The separation of church and state necessarily means the separation of religion and politics.

9. Churches are man-made organizations that you can take or leave. They are inherently corrupt and compromising of true spirituality, and the larger they are the more suspicious we should be.
10. The Jesus of the New Testament is a historically inaccurate fabrication which should not be believed.

This is really the heart of removing sin from not only our vocabulary but our lives. Call what is sin not a sin. It's the great seduction of the serpent in the Garden of Eden. When you believe a lie, you are rejecting the truth. When there is no truth, you forget how to blush.

Or to even care.

Bleeding Two-Year-Olds

Much has been written of China's economic prowess and growing influence over the past two decades in the midst of a global economic meltdown. Many of us can still remember marveling at the 2008 Opening Ceremonies of the Summer Olympics in Beijing.

Let's face it—China has been on a roll. But money and public relations aren't everything.

There are also two-year-old girls.

Wang Yue was a toddler who was run over—twice—and ignored by at least eighteen people as she lay in a pool of her own blood in a Guandong market in October 2011. The horrifying indifference was captured on a video watched by millions around the world, forcing the country's leaders to acknowledge that the country's "cultural development" lags behind its other accomplishments.

After a four-day closed-door meeting, the over 200-member Central Committee of the Community Party issued a communiqué calling for the country to build a "powerful socialist culture" that would involve "significantly improving the nation's ideological and moral qualities." Senior Politburo member Li Changchun was quoted as saying "venality, lack of integrity and moral anomalies" were on the rise in Chinese society.

Wang Yue's case was just the latest scandal in a country that has become increasingly accustomed to astonishing stories of wanton corruption, internet scams, tainted baby food, and even child abductions with official involvement. As Mark MacKinnon writes in Canada's *Globe and Mail*,

> Many see the Communist Party as having created the vacuum it now seeks to fill. Religion was crushed following the country's 1949 Revolution, and the ideology that was supposed to replace it—Maoism—went out the window when the country undertook its economic reforms of the 1980s and 1990s . . . they say they have a socialist value system, but no one knows what that means.[11]

Or as Bo Zhiyue, an expert on Chinese politics at the National University of Singapore, observed, "No one believes in Marxism any more. Confucianism is not being revived, and the so-called Western universal values are not being accepted."[12]

Sadly, little Yueyue, as the girl is known in China, lost the battle in intensive care and died from brain and organ failure.

Hopefully not like her country.

And hopefully not like ours.

Marriage and Family

11

Just Not into Marriage

Men resemble the times
More than they resemble their fathers.

Arab proverb[1]

When Prince William and Kate Middleton announced their engagement, an interesting fact was barely mentioned: they were already living together outside of marriage.

Kate had moved in with William at his home in North Wales while he trained to be an RAF search-and-rescue pilot. I recall watching television when William and Kate's premarital living arrangements were airily mentioned, and one reporter in the U.K. commented how wonderful it was that we live in a day when such matters are inconsequential.

He's right about one thing. Today, such matters are.

We're just not into marriage.

According to the *Wall Street Journal*, for the first time since the US began tallying marriages, more Americans of prime marrying age have stayed single rather than tie the knot. According to the Census Bureau, the proportion of married adults of all ages was only 52 percent in

2009, down from 72.2 percent in 1960—the lowest percentage since the US began tracking statistics in 1880.[2] In 2011 the Pew Research Center released a report that the share of all US adults who were married dropped another percentage point and that new marriages dropped a sharp 5 percent from the previous year.[3] "A slowdown in marriage rates doesn't mean the end of cohabiting relationships," noted Conor Dougherty in the *Wall Street Journal* report. "As marriage rates have fallen, the number of adults living together has skyrocketed." More specifically, according to other Pew Research Center findings, cohabitation has nearly doubled since 1990.[4]

According to a 2011 report published by the National Marriage Project, an initiative at the University of Virginia, the number of unmarried Americans who live together and have children has increased twelvefold since 1970. The report goes on to state that children are now more likely to have unmarried parents than divorced ones.[5] According to a study from the University of Missouri, the path from courtship to marriage is being further altered by a growing number of young American adults who are engaging in what's called "stay-over relationships," in which they spend three or more nights together each week while still having the option of returning to their own homes.[6] So it's little wonder that Mexico City lawmakers are considering a proposal for short-term marriage contracts. Couples will be able to choose the length of their marriage, with a minimum length of two years, and then renew the contract if they stay happy.[7]

And divorce? Now even the end of marriage is losing its social stigma and is becoming mainstream—even celebrated. Arianna Huffington, founder of the news site *Huffington Post*, launched a site on all things related to divorce (huffpostdivorce.com) with famed movie director and screenwriter Nora Ephron as editor at large. Its tagline? "Marriage comes and goes, but divorce is forever." The implication is that there is life—good life—after divorce. Commenting on the site, life coach Jill Brooke acknowledged on NBC's *Today Show* that due to the mainstreaming of divorce and our culture of immediate gratification, many are divorcing too quickly. The pursuit of personal happiness has trumped the commitment to family.[8] So it's no surprise that one of the increasingly common pictures on Facebook is from "divorce parties."

I recall logging on to the opening page of America Online one day when the feature tease was, "Live Together and Save Money," suggesting that I should "go the domestic partner route." One click away was a collection of articles headlined "Living in Sin and Loving the Savings." The short, descriptive paragraph encouraging my exploration of the many features read, "More and more couples are shacking up rather than getting hitched. And why not? These days, live-ins are eligible for many new financial perks."[9]

And that's the key line: "And why not?"

The guiding motif of the modern world when it comes to alternatives to marriage is why *not*. Marriage is increasingly seen as a mere social construct, and thus plastic. This means it can be shaped and formed into whatever we desire it to be—including discarded altogether. There is no sense that marriage is something permanent and binding, rooted in the very fabric of creation. "Even the most casual observer or critic of marriage would acknowledge that the institution is too often held in very low cultural esteem," observes Jim Daly, president of Focus on the Family. "From television to movies to music, the bonds of matrimony are often lampooned as chains that bind and confine as opposed to the great anchor of stability God intended them to be."[10]

The Crumbling State of Marriage

- For the first time since the US began tallying marriages, more Americans of prime marrying age have stayed single rather than tied the knot.
- Proportion of married adults of all ages was 52 percent in 2009, down from 72.2 percent in 1960—the lowest percentage since the US began tracking in 1880.
- Cohabitation in the US has nearly doubled since 1990.
- The number of unmarried Americans who live together and have children has increased twelvefold since 1970.
- Children are now more likely to have unmarried parents than divorced ones.

One of the more insightful comments on the recent data documenting the decline of marriage comes from Ross Douthat at the *New York Times*:

> The long-running culture war arguments about how to structure family life (Should marriage be reserved for heterosexuals? Is abstinence or "safe sex" the most responsible way to navigate the premarital landscape?) looks increasingly irrelevant. . . . This, in turn, may be remembered as the great tragedy of the culture war: While [some] Americans battle over what marriage should mean, much of the country may be abandoning the institution entirely.[11]

Why Marriage Matters

As Glenn Stanton and Bill Maier note, marriage is never simply about the couple; it's about the larger community. It is an agreement between the couple and the larger society. It is precisely this relationship, and the concern for the larger society, that causes churches and government to get involved at all.

Every society needs marriage to:

- regulate sexuality, keeping it confined to committed, loving, exclusive relationships
- socialize men, channeling their sexual and masculine energy in community-building ways
- protect women from being exploited by men
- ensure that children grow up with biologically connected mothers and fathers

Marriage has served these purposes in all known human civilizations by bringing men and women together in permanent, exclusive relationships.[12]

Marriage is also the key to personal happiness and fulfillment. As social scientist James Q. Wilson explains,

> Married people are happier than unmarried ones of the same age, not only in the United States, but in at least seventeen other countries where similar inquiries have been made. And there seem to be good

reasons for that happiness. People who are married not only have higher incomes and enjoy greater emotional support, they tend to be healthier. Married people live longer than unmarried ones, not only in the United States, but abroad.[13]

As Stanton and Maier note, another survey of fourteen thousand adults measured over a ten-year period found that marital status was one of the strongest indicators of happiness, with the married being the happiest, generally, and the divorced being the most unhappy, even behind the widowed.[14]

And children? One out of every four children in the United States is being raised by a single parent.[15] Yet the child advocacy organization Center for Law and Social Policy (CLASP) has reported: "Most researchers now agree that . . . studies support the notion that, on average, children do best when raised by their two married biological parents."[16]

That's a bit of an understatement.

A landmark study published in the *American Journal of Psychiatry* found that 90 percent of children from divorced homes suffered from an acute sense of shock when the separation occurred, including profound grieving and irrational fears. Fifty percent reported feelings of rejection and abandonment. Sixty-six percent experienced yearning for the absent parent with an intensity that researchers described as overwhelming. Nearly half were even more unhappy five years after the divorce than they had been at the eighteen-month mark. In other words, time didn't heal their wounds.[17]

Gay Marriage

In many ways, it is the devaluation of marriage that has brought gay marriage to the surface. Many observers have noted that the homosexual community is not as interested in the right to marry as they are in legitimizing their lifestyle—and marriage would be that cultural affirmation. Because marriage has become so porous in terms of definition and nature, it lends itself to precisely such use.

But regardless, the gay marriage debate reveals the changing attitude toward marriage itself. As David Coolidge of the Institute on Religion and Public Life observes, there are two worldviews at hand.[18]

The first can be called the *complementarity* model. This assumes that the universe was created with an objective moral order, that the two sexes are part of that order, and that marriage is the fundamental social institution by which we unite our lives in family and kinship relationships. This is a model that is virtually universal in traditional societies.

Yet what is being proposed, Coolidge argues, is the *choice* model. This worldview assumes that individuals create their own truths and their own values. Sexuality has no intrinsic purpose—it's just an opportunity for pleasure or intimacy. Family structure is as pliable as Play-Doh, and any form is acceptable. Under this view, the right to marry is no more than the right to participate in state-defined benefits.

The choice between the two views is clear, and so is the impact on our world. If we go with the choice model, we are saying there is no objective moral order and marriage is no more than a human invention—ours to change, redefine, even discard. In other words, the legalization of homosexual marriage would quickly erode any sense of the traditional family in our culture. The words *husband* and *wife*, *mother* and *father* would quickly lose their meaning. God's roles, rooted in creation itself, would be abandoned. (In fact, the State Department has announced that the words *mother* and *father* are being removed from US passport applications and replaced with gender-neutral terminology.)

Further, it will open the floodgates to increased redefinitions. Already there are lawsuits attempting to build off the idea of gay marriage to justify polygamy and many other alternatives to one-man/one-woman unions. This is why Timothy George observes,

> At stake in the debate is the very nature of marriage itself. Thinking biblically does not allow us to regard marriage as merely prudential or preferential (I like strawberry, you like pistachio), but as a covenantal union of one man and one woman established by God for a purpose that transcends itself. Marriage is not a *right* to be defended or exploited but rather a union of one man and one woman offering their lives to one another in service to the human community.[19]

In February of 2011 the attorney general announced that the Justice Department would no longer defend the full constitutionality of the

1996 Defense of Marriage Act. Specifically section 3, which says that in interpreting federal law, "the word 'marriage' means only a legal union between one man and one woman as husband and wife."[20] At the time of this writing, same-sex marriage is legal in six states.

Who Wants to Live with Someone for Eighty Years?

In a recent interview, actress Cameron Diaz made it quite clear that she is content to be—and intent on being—a serial dater. In an interview with the U.K.'s *Stylist* magazine, she said, "I think the big misconception in our society is that we're supposed to meet the one when we're 18, and we're supposed to get married to them and love them for the rest of our lives. Bulls**t."

"Who would want to be with the same person for 80 years?" she added. Diaz maintains it's best to break it up a bit. She thinks that people get freaked out about long-term commitments and marriage and the thought of spending two or three decades living, eating, and sleeping with one person.

So what does Diaz intend to do? "Have someone for five years and another person for another five years," she said.[21] Because while she admits that there are those few people who may happen to find a lifelong love, even they may not want to necessarily live together their whole lives. Because who knows when someone else may come along to stir up those same feelings of love.

And according to Diaz, there's nothing wrong with that.

12

Pornification

Every blush is a cause for new blushes.
David Hume, 1741[1]

In an article in the *New York Times*, Stephanie Rosenbloom examined how a word that originated in the middle ages has emerged from a schoolyard barb to become commonplace in popular culture, marketing, and casual conversation.

It's the word *slut*.

"She is the one who will go home with you, the sure bet, the kind of girl you can lie down with and then walk all over. She is ogled, envied, and often ostracized."[2]

In his duet with the rapper Eminem, Nate Dogg describes his hunt for "a big old slut" in the single "Shake That." The ample-bosomed puppet in the Broadway musical *Avenue Q* is called Lucy the Slut. Novelty shops and websites sell slut lip balm, bubble bath, soap, and lotion. A cocktail is known as the red-headed slut. A teenager on MTV's *Laguna Beach: The Real Orange County* demanded that a rival admit she was a slut, which she did.

Rosenbloom notes that the word *slut* is tossed around so often and so casually that many teenagers use it affectionately and in jest among their friends, even incorporating it into their instant messenger screen names. Like *queer* and *pimp* before it, the word *slut* seems to be moving away from its meaning as a slur. Karell Roxas, a senior editor at Gurl.com, a website that addresses issues that affect teenage girls, notes that today teenagers say, "Hi, slut!" the way earlier generations said, "Hi, chick!" Even among adults, we use phrases like "coffee slut" or "TV slut" to intimate voraciousness.[3]

Our Fascination with *Slut*

- Nate Dogg sings of his hunt for "a big old slut" in the single "Shake That"
- The Broadway musical *Avenue Q* has an ample-bosomed puppet named Lucy the Slut
- You can purchase slut products from lip balm and bubble bath to soap and lotion
- There's a cocktail called the red-headed slut
- Stripping and pole dancing have now become a form of exercise

---

Altoosa Rubenstein, editor in chief of *Seventeen* magazine, notes that "Today, 'slut,' even 'ho' . . . is used in a fun way, a positive way."[4] Rosenbloom notes that cultivating an exhibitionistic, slutty appearance—donning the trappings of promiscuity—has been a growing influence on fashion and popular culture for a decade. Women wear T-shirts with provocative slogans. Stripping and pole dancing is an *au courant* way to exercise.[5]

The "taming of the slur" is perhaps one of the more telling developments in our culture's moral slide, and perhaps one of the more influential. Leora Tanenbaum, author of *Slut! Growing Up Female with a Bad Reputation*, interviewed more than one hundred women between the ages of fourteen and sixty-six who had been pigeonholed as sluts. She found that the label can be a self-fulfilling prophecy, leading to greater promiscuity.[6]

Now that the label has been self-imposed on an entire generation, it even marks one of our most popular holidays.

The Trick in the Treat

I grew up in a day when Halloween was little more than pumpkins, fall festivals, hayrides, and dressing up as a pirate or a farmer to go trick-or-treating. That is what it held for my now post-Halloween-age children as well. As a result, I've had a built-in resistance to those Christians who bash October 31 as a pagan festival that followers of Christ have no business supporting, much less engaging. I know its history, but few celebrations in our day are free of pagan roots, and the idea that donning a costume and receiving a mini-Snickers bar was an invitation to the occult was ludicrous to my thinking.

I still hold to the childlike fun the night can hold, but I no longer view the day *itself* as innocuous. For example, in an article in the *New York Times* titled, "Good Girls Go Bad, for a Day," the changing nature of women's Halloween costumes in the last several years is candidly marked. Little Red Riding Hood, in her thigh-highs and miniskirt, does not seem en route to her grandmother's house. Goldilocks, in a snug bodice and platform heels, gives the impression she has been sleeping in everyone's bed. And then there is the witch wearing little more than a Laker Girl uniform, a fairy who appears to shop at Victoria's Secret, and a cowgirl with a skirt the size of a—well, you get the point.

The images "are more strip club than storybook." It's a wonder, the article adds, that "gyms do not have 'get in shape for Halloween' specials." Of course experts are often trotted out to speak of this as the *empowering* of women as they embrace their sexuality, and they look for deep and positive meanings in the evolution of Cinderella from virgin to vixen. But take a walk through your neighborhood mall's costume store—with the prominent sign out front saying, "No one under 18 allowed without a parent"—and you can cut through the sociological analysis. So we dress as Little Bo *Peep Show* and Miss Foul Play. It is, as comedian Carlos Mencia jokes, "Dress like a whore day."[7]

Pornification

Let's coin a term, shall we?

You've heard of commercialization and bureaucratization.

How about *pornification*?

It is as though we have sexualized everything. Can you name something that is sold that hasn't been sexualized in terms of marketing strategy? Would the average person even suspect that GoDaddy.com is about licensing Web domains instead of an actual porn site? Would we ever make the connection between an allusion to phone sex and buying car insurance?

Perhaps the most brazen example of this comes from PETA (People for the Ethical Treatment of Animals), the animal rights group known for everything from celebrities posing nude for its anti-fur campaign to scantily clad women having an erotic moment with a vegetable (to support veganism). Now PETA has launched an XXX porn site to raise awareness of veganism—all in an effort to protect animals. The site will feature adult pornography as well as graphic images of animals being tortured or mistreated. Yes, porn will be used in a public service campaign.[8]

We all know about the hardcore pornography available on the internet. This has led thoughtful parents to install filters and take other actions to protect their children from the seedy ghettoes of cyberspace. But the pervasive sexualization of our culture is far from confined to the Web. A new study has shown that most kids aren't exposed to sexual content on the internet as much as they are through television and music, an area where most parents have turned a blind eye. Between 16 and 25 percent of children say they are exposed to sexual material on the internet, while 75 percent say they are exposed to it on TV and 69 percent in their music.[9]

As Frank Rich wrote in the *New York Times Magazine*, "Pornography is no longer a sideshow to the mainstream . . . it is the mainstream."[10] Or as Juliann Garey notes, "Strippers are showing up with such frequency . . . that they're no longer shocking—and that's the problem. What once provoked some kind of response—embarrassment, outrage, anxiety, titillation—now seems routine."[11] Pamela Paul writes of a "pornified America" where pornography has become a part of our daily lives.[12] It's on the covers of mainstream men's magazines; in the promotion of music, movie, and television celebrities; and in the advice columns of women's magazines.

There is no longer a stigma; the one thing that is guaranteed to the woman who lands on the cover of *Sports Illustrated*'s famed swimsuit issue is a guest spot on the *Today Show*.

Is Porn Really That Big a Deal?

Is it really that bad that porn has become such a big part of our lives?

In her book *Pornified*, Pamela Paul responds with a resounding "Yes!" As porn becomes more pervasive, Paul argues that it has changed our marriages and families as well as our children's understanding of sex and sexuality. Her portraits are riveting:

- Rob, who insists that his girlfriend look and behave like a porn star in and out of bed
- Charlie, who spends hours cruising porn sites and setting up meetings with women and couples he befriends in chat rooms, while telling his wife that he's just working late on the computer
- Jonah, a fan of violent, hardcore porn, who introduces tamer porn to his fiancée in an effort to revive their troubled sex life
- Abby, who discovers her husband's hidden box of CDs of child porn images downloaded from the internet
- preteen girls who start their own pornography websites
- teenage boys, mimicking porn, who videotape themselves having sex with an apparently unconscious girl[13]

Where Are Children Being Exposed to Sexual Content?

As reported by *USA Today*:

> Between 16 and 25 percent of children say they are exposed to sexual material on the internet, while 75 percent say they are exposed to it on TV and 69 percent in their music.

And make no mistake about how pervasive porn has become. According to compiled numbers from various news and research organizations, every second, $3,075.64 is being spent on pornography. Every second, 28,258 internet users are viewing pornography. In that same second, 372 internet users are typing adult search terms into search engines. Every thirty-nine minutes, a new pornographic video is being created in the US—and it's big business. The pornography industry has larger revenues than Microsoft, Google, Amazon, eBay, Yahoo, Apple, and Netflix combined.[14]

The ubiquitous nature of porn is new to our culture and to human sexuality, but it is already becoming clear that porn is highly addictive in nature. As a result, not only can it begin to dominate a life, but it can demand ever-increasing levels of exposure and ever-increasing degrees of debauchery to continue to stimulate. Studies are beginning to show that the effects of porn on men is more than temporary sexual stimulation: as they see women treated as objects, they begin to treat women that way. They become more sexually aggressive, leading to date rapes and expected hook-ups. For married men, porn quickly becomes a substitute for sexual intimacy with their spouse.

Now imagine its effect on children.

The online sex magazine *Nerve* recently published an interview with an eighth-grade girl called "Z" about internet pornography.[15]

> NERVE: *Have you ever seen any pornography on the internet?*
> Z: Obviously.
> NERVE: How old were you would you estimate when you first saw porn?
> Z: I guess ten, but that was because there were pop-ups, like advertisements, sh** like that.
> NERVE: So do you know anyone who's really into internet porn?
> Z: Basically all my friends are.
> NERVE: Are you?
> Z: Yeah. I'm not like ashamed to say that. Most of the time the way my friends look at it it's not like, "Oh my God, that's so hot." It's like, "Yeah, that's all right." I sort of like gothic porn.

Pornography, in one form or another, so permeates our culture that we are not even aware of its surrounding presence, much less its demeaning and degrading effect. As a result, we think of it as normal.

But it's not normal.

C. S. Lewis writes,

> You can get a large audience together for a strip-tease act, that is, to watch a girl undress on the stage. Now suppose you came to a country

where you could fill a theatre by simply bringing a covered plate on to the stage and then slowly lifting the cover so as to let everyone see, just before the lights went out, that it contained a mutton chop or a bit of bacon, would you not think that in that country something had gone wrong with the appetite for food? And would not anyone who had grown up in a different world think there was something equally queer about the state of the sex instinct among us?[16]

Yes, they would.

13

Modern Family

Homosexuality is assuredly no advantage, but it is
nothing to be ashamed of, no vice, no degradation.

Sigmund Freud[1]

Actress Jada Pinkett Smith was honored as the Artist of the Year by
the Harvard Foundation for Intercultural and Race Relations at the
foundation's twentieth annual Cultural Rhythms show. In a speech
many students considered inspirational and motivating, Pinkett Smith
gave a warm, teary thanks and then shared life lessons with the audience. "Don't let anybody define who you are," she said. "Don't let
them put you in a box." She told them about her childhood with teenage parents both addicted to heroin, but triumphantly proclaimed, "I
can stand here on this stage and say that I've proven them all wrong."

She then addressed issues regarding the roles of men and women
today, specifically encouraging women to fight against the idea that
choosing a career means having to choose against marriage and family. "Women, you can have . . . a loving man, devoted husband, loving
children, . . . [and a] career. . . . All you have to do is want it." Pinkett
Smith has been married to actor Will Smith since 1997 and is the
mother of two children.[2]

Though the Cultural Rhythms show is designed to feature culturally unique forms of artistic expression along the lines of varying forms of music, the Bisexual, Gay, Lesbian, Transgender, and Supporters Alliance (BGLTSA) were offended that Pinkett Smith's comments seemed specific to heterosexual relationships. Conceding that there was nothing in her remarks that was remotely homophobic, the BGLTSA nonetheless expressed concern that her content was "extremely heteronormative"—meaning her comments implied that standard sexual relationships are only between males and females, making BGLTSA members feel uncomfortable.[3]

How times have changed.

Seismic Change

No other change in public opinion has been as swift as the one regarding homosexuality. It has simply been breathtaking.

What once was in the closet is now a parade.

What once was whispered behind backs in derision is now the focus of sitcoms.

What once was publicly denounced is now deemed by many as essential to embrace.

And it happened in less than a generation.

Indeed, the events of even a few short weeks can be seismic in nature, occurring so fast that even the most seasoned of pundits struggle to stay abreast of their full meaning. The end of 2010 and the beginning of 2011 was that way.

- In August 2010, ABC's hit comedy *Modern Family*—prominently featuring a same-sex couple—wins the Emmy for outstanding comedy series.
- In late December, the Senate passes a repeal of the seventeen-year-old ban known as "Don't Ask, Don't Tell," now allowing gays to serve openly in the military.
- The Southern Poverty Law Center classified as "hate groups" several Christian organizations that have taken a stance against the acceptance of gay marriage or that have simply gone public

with a stance against homosexuality as a morally acceptable lifestyle.

- On Thursday, February 11, 2011, after talks with gay rights organizations, including GLAAD (the Gay and Lesbian Alliance Against Defamation), Facebook adds civil unions and domestic partnerships to the list of relationships that its users can pick from to best describe their romantic status. And as one media adviser put it, "As Facebook goes, so goes the world."[4]

- In a historic shift on gay rights, the Obama administration announces on February 23, 2011, that it believes the Constitution forbids unequal treatment of gays and lesbians in almost all cases, and specifically when it comes to federal benefits for legally married same-sex couples. As a result, the Justice Department will no longer oppose legal challenges to the Defense of Marriage Act, passed by Congress in 1996, which bars the federal government from recognizing same-sex marriages or extending them the same benefits as heterosexual couples.

- New York becomes the sixth and largest state to legalize gay marriage.

- California passes a bill requiring the contributions of gay heroes and role models to be included in history classes and textbooks.

- For the first time in history, a majority of Americans support same-sex marriage.[5]

Whew.

To put this into perspective, when President Bill Clinton signed the Defense of Marriage Act into law in 1996, the first episode of the gay-friendly sitcom *Will and Grace* hadn't even aired. As Clinton began his second term, only 27 percent of the population approved of same-sex marriage.[6]

This has led some Christians not to call for moral courage and a stand against a redefinition of sexual mores, but to call for a "Great Gay Awakening" that affirms homosexuality as a lifestyle. The idea is that since we're losing the cultural battle, we should give in and find a new moral front. Jay Bakker, son of Jim Bakker and the late Tammy Faye Messner, even declared that homosexuality should not be considered a sin. Agreeing with Bakker was Tony Jones, theologian in residence at Minnesota's Solomon's Porch, and Peggy Campolo, wife of evangelist Tony Campolo. Author Brian McLaren condemned the Christian preoccupation with homosexuality as "fundasexuality."[7]

Culture Shift

Three things have fueled this rapid cultural acceptance.

First, there is the treatment of homosexuality in the media. One of the great powers of the media is its ability to normalize a behavior, attitude, or belief. The heart of this power is how it makes us feel. When you can get someone to feel a certain way, you can lead them to a certain belief *through* those feelings. If I'm led to feel sympathetically toward a person's perspective or life situation, then that colors my moral assessment of his or her life choices.

Then there is the repetition media provides, putting certain alternate choices or lifestyles before us over and over again until we have become desensitized to such decisions and accept those choices and lifestyles as normal. Combining feeling and repetition, if the repetitive behavior is exhibited through a character that is particularly likable, the influence is greater still. With homosexuality, this has been achieved through such sitcoms as *Will and Grace* and, more recently, *Modern Family* and *Glee*. As George Lucas, one of the most successful filmmakers in Hollywood history, once said, "For better or worse . . . films and television tell us the way we conduct our lives, what is right and wrong."[8]

Never has that been more true than with homosexuality.

A second reason for the rapid cultural change has been a very active and organized movement to denounce and demonize anything opposing homosexuality in the name of tolerance and even civil rights. It is not simply a matter of wanting the freedom to openly pursue a homosexual lifestyle, but the demand that any denunciation of such a lifestyle be eliminated from culture. This is such a vast area to explore that I will simply give two examples as windows into this dynamic. The first comes from a recent political election cycle but begins with psychology.

There is a clear divide between the American Psychological Association (APA) and the American Association of Christian Counselors (AACC) on what is known as "reparative therapy," or so-called gay-to-straight counseling. Until 1973 the APA listed homosexuality as one of its official mental disorders. Now they say that "efforts to change sexual orientation are unlikely to be successful and involve some risk of harm." Further, there is enormous anger from the homosexual community toward any type of reparative therapy because it intimates there is something inherently wrong with the homosexual lifestyle that can be "fixed."

What a Difference a Year Makes

- August 2010—*Modern Family*, ABC's hit comedy featuring a same-sex couple, wins the Emmy for outstanding comedy series
- December 2010—The US Senate passes a repeal of "Don't Ask, Don't Tell," allowing gays to serve openly in the military
- January 2011—The Southern Poverty Law Center classifies as "hate groups" several Christian organizations that have taken stances they feel are against homosexuality
- February 2011—Facebook adds civil unions and domestic partnerships to the list of relationships under their romantic status choices
- February 23, 2011—The Justice Department will no longer oppose challenges to the Defense of Marriage Act after decision from the Obama administration
- June 2011—New York becomes the sixth and largest state to legalize gay marriage
- July 2011—California passes a bill requiring the contributions of gay heroes and role models to be included in history classes and textbooks
- May 2011—For the first time in history, the majority of Americans support same-sex marriage

The AACC, which has 50,000 members, supports reparative therapy "on biblical, ethical, and legal grounds" for patients who have "a genuine desire to be set free of homosexual attractions." The goal is "heterosexual relations and marriage or life-long sexual celibacy."[9]

The husband of US Representative and former presidential candidate Michele Bachmann runs a Christian counseling center. Truth Wins Out (a national nonprofit group dedicated to fighting "anti-gay religious extremism") sought out former patients of Dr. Bachmann's clinic to see how they were treated. The group also sent its communications director, John Becker, who is gay, to the clinic to pose as a patient seeking to become heterosexual. He recorded his conversation with a therapist on two hidden cameras and an audio device.

So what, exactly, was discovered?

Timothy Wiertzema, a licensed marriage and family therapist with the center, said he would be willing to work with Mr. Becker but did not aggressively press him to change his sexuality. When asked about the possibility of "getting rid of it completely," Mr. Wiertzema replied that some people had, but that for others homosexuality simply "becomes manageable." Verdict from Truth Wins Out? "What we found was reasonably professional with a skewed point of view toward homosexuality being a negative and no offering of hope that it is something positive."[10]

The media went into a feeding frenzy. The *Today Show* on NBC ran a report that made it sound like Bachmann's husband had committed a scandalous act by possibly suggesting homosexuality could be treated. The *New York Times* ran the headline, "Christian Counseling by Hopeful's Spouse Prompts Questions."[11]

Translation: No matter how well handled, what will not be tolerated is any sense that homosexuality as a lifestyle is wrong. Bachmann's cultural sin was to suggest that homosexuality as a lifestyle was less than ideal, or at least worthy of treatment if someone so wishes.

That's it.

"Either you're with them or you're a hater," said Maggie Gallagher, the president of the Institute for Marriage and Public Policy, about gay rights advocates. "They're trying to exclude you from the public square."[12]

Another example of such exclusion comes from a high school in Wisconsin. The editorial page of the school newspaper ran two contrasting opinion pieces about gay families who adopt children. One was in favor of such adoptions, the other raised questions, concerns, and opposition. The opposing piece was subsequently called "hateful" and blamed for potential teen suicides and provocation of bullying. When a single gay family told them it should never have been run, school officials apologized and agreed the article was offensive.

But was it?

Here's what the student actually wrote: "If one is a practicing Christian, Jesus states in the Bible that homosexuality is (a) detestable act and sin which makes adopting wrong for homosexuals because you would be raising the child in a sin-filled environment. . . . A child adopted into homosexuality will get confused because everyone else will have two different-gendered parents that can give them the correct amount of motherly nurturing and fatherly structure. In a Christian society, allowing homosexual couples to adopt is an abomination."

There is little doubt that the words *detestable*, *sin*, and *abomination* are strong. There is also little doubt that bullying is wrong. But this was the student's opinion. And it was an opinion page, with an article supporting homosexuality running by its side. So while their opinion was distasteful to some, the student journalists were exercising their constitutional right to free speech.[13]

So who, exactly, was discriminated against?

Primary Reasons for the Cultural Acceptance of Homosexuality

1. Treatment of homosexuality in the media that helps to normalize this lifestyle through programs such as *Will and Grace, Modern Family*, and *Glee*.
2. A very active and organized movement to denounce and demonize anything opposing homosexuality in the name of tolerance and even civil rights.
3. Targeted approaches to appeal to popular sensibility and our views on morality, specifically by focusing on the rights of the individual and then shifting to making opposition to homosexuality, not homosexuality itself, what is immoral.

The third reason for the rapid cultural acceptance of homosexuality is the very specific and targeted approaches designed to appeal to popular sensibility and views on morality. It began with a focus on the rights of the individual, in an attempt to cast the acceptance of homosexuality in the same way as equality for women and the civil rights movement of the sixties. When that seemed to achieve all it could, the tactic then became lifting up the love and commitment that exists between homosexual couples. Regardless of the approach, the tactic is the same and quite ironic: let's make opposition to homosexuality, not homosexuality itself, what is immoral. After all, how can people be against love and commitment?

It's a deft move.

And it's working. Or should I say, "And it has worked."

So complete is the culture shift that many religious leaders are advocating dropping any and all public opposition to things such as gay marriage in order to put their efforts into religious freedom. In other words, they want to make sure that any and all future legislation protects those who oppose gay marriage from being persecuted and prosecuted for their convictions.

14

Regarding Gender

We may be about to enter into a posthuman future,
in which technology will give us the capacity gradu-
ally to alter that essence over time. . . . But this kind
of freedom will be different from all other freedoms
that people have previously enjoyed. . . . We should
do it with our eyes open.

Francis Fukuyama[1]

I have long told my graduate students that the doctrine of humanity
is by far the most pressing doctrine of our day. This is because it is
the area of Christian thought that is most challenged by the world in
which we live, and the nature of those challenges tends to leave most
Christians bereft of any sense of knowing how to think.

When it comes to the idea of being human, there are three foundational statements that must be made, rooted in the account of creation
itself: (1) We have been made. We were created, personally, by God.
(2) We were made in the image of God. This means that when God
made us, he put something of himself in us—a spark of the divine.
Because we are made in the image of God, we have a soul that is able
to respond and relate to God. Nothing else in all of creation carries

that standing, and that makes human life sacred. (3) We were created male and female. The Bible says that when God created human beings, he intentionally created diversity. He purposefully made us a race of men and a race of women. Within this diversity is individual diversity, as each human being is distinct from every other.

But this raises many, many questions, including:

- When does human life begin and end?
- What should we take upon ourselves to do with its beginning and ending?
- What are we allowed to do in terms of shaping our bodies and personalities?
- What about the duplication of human beings?

In fairness, there is no rich historical vein of theological reflection to pull from, at least in terms of our current cultural conversation. Try to find a reflection from Origen or Athanasius, Luther or Melanchthon, Barth or Brunner that speaks to stem-cell research, human cloning, or homosexual rights. Yes, there is much on what constitutes humanity, the nature of humanity in relation to God, and the boundaries of sexual ethics—but the issues of our day pose questions that leave previous theological discourse sorely lacking. As the first five centuries hammered out Christology and later generations tackled everything from the Holy Spirit to revelation, ours may be the day that is forced to examine the doctrine of humanity in ways that serve the church for years to come.

And the challenge has quickly gone to one of the core ideas related to human identity.

That God created us male and female.

Gender and Sex

Recent news headlines have been startling.

- A husband and wife are raising their four-month-old son without revealing his (or is it her?) gender.

- An androgynous Australian model works both the male and female runways at the Paris fashion shows.
- A J. Crew catalog drew national attention for featuring a young boy with his toenails painted pink.

Are we nearing the end of gender?

It's a fascinating question, raised by a report on National Public Radio titled "The End of Gender."[2] *Gender* is defined as the "behavioral, cultural, or psychological traits typically associated with one sex." In other words, the attitudes, actions, dress, and sensibilities that go with being a boy or being a girl. Or as NPR put it, gender is the "cultural expectations" that come with a particular sex. Gender is distinct from the nature of sexuality, which is an important distinction in the current cultural dialogue. While the differences inherent between the sexes are beyond question, the growing movement seems to be toward the removal of gender from the cultural equation.

So we have a high school prom court in Michigan that goes "gender-free," without prom kings or queens, after denying a transgender student the homecoming king crown the year before.

Then there is East Tennessee State University, which is exploring gender-neutral housing for its students (following the lead of Stanford, the University of Michigan, Rutgers, and others). UCLA is considering a plan to put young men and women in the same dorm room, calling it "gender inclusive" dorm life, acknowledging that most requests have been received from "transgender students asking to live with a student of the gender to which they are transitioning."[3]

Even the State Department now issues passports in gender-neutral terms, referring to "Parent One" or "Parent Two" instead of "father" or "mother."

Not to mention the rush toward gender-neutral translations of the Bible.

You've probably heard of the term "metrosexual." A metrosexual is a guy you find deep in the hair-care aisle or in the salon having his nails buffed to the perfect shine while he's checking out the latest fashion magazines. He's a sensitive, well-educated urban dweller in touch with his feminine side. He loves to shop, wear jewelry, and fill his bathroom counter with moisturizers—and maybe even makeup.

In other words, he embodies a new definition of what it means to be a man, one that borrows heavily from what it means to be a woman, and combines it into a new identity.

What began as a fashion trend is now erupting into culture in ways that are challenging the very nature of human sexuality.

Headlines on Gender

- A husband and wife are raising their four-month-old son without revealing his (or is it her?) gender.
- An androgynous Australian model works both the male and female runways at the Paris fashion shows.
- A. J. Crew catalog drew national attention for featuring a young boy with his toenails painted pink.
- A high school prom court in Michigan went "gender-free" without prom kings or queens after denying a transgender student the homecoming king crown the year before.
- East Tennessee University explores gender-neutral housing for its students following the lead of Stanford, the University of Michigan, Rutgers, and others.
- UCLA is considering a plan to put young men and women in the same dorm room, calling it "gender inclusive" dorm life.
- The State Department issues passports in gender-neutral terms, referring to "Parent One" and "Parent Two" instead of "father" or "mother."

Does Sex Matter?

In his book *Taking Sex Differences Seriously*, University of Virginia professor Dr. Steven Rhoads writes about an incident that took place in 1966.[4] A botched circumcision left one of two male identical twins without a full male organ. A leading sex psychologist at Johns Hopkins University persuaded the parents to raise that toddler as a female. They completed the castration, constructed what appeared from the outside to be female genitalia, and called him Brenda. They raised him as a girl, and even gave him female steroids to mimic female pubertal growth and feminization.

All seemed to be well.

Time magazine called the case "strong support" for the view that masculine and feminine behavior can be altered. A 1979 textbook used the case to discuss how human gender identity was flexible and plastic, and how being male or female was the product of social learning and conditioning. Numerous psychology and sociology texts cited the case as proof that sex roles are basically learned.

But people didn't follow the case through to the end. Even with the injection of female hormones, the absence of male hormones coming from testicles, and being raised as a female, Brenda did not turn out as Brenda. In the early 1990s, a team of researchers caught up with the boy who had been turned into a girl to see how "she" was doing.

They found that "she" was no longer Brenda. "She" was now David—working in a slaughterhouse, married to a woman, and the adoptive father of three children.

At the age of fourteen, Brenda had decided to start living as a male, and at fifteen was told that "she" indeed had been born as a boy. She then announced that she had always felt like a male and wanted to become one again. Brenda was given a mastectomy, male hormones, and constructed genitalia.

When researchers dug further, they found that:

- The first time Brenda was put in a dress, he pulled it off.
- When given a jump rope, he wanted to tie people up with it or whip them with it.
- At nine, he bought a toy machine gun when he was supposed to buy an umbrella.
- His toy sewing machine went untouched because he preferred to build forts and play with dump trucks.
- He was never interested in makeup, but instead wanted to shave with his father.
- On a trip to New York City, he found himself attracted to the Rockettes.
- He even felt the urge to urinate standing up.

Because of this, researchers at Johns Hopkins felt they should go back and study other children who had undergone similar operations;

boys who, for whatever reason, were born without full male organs, had then been fully castrated, and were raised as girls. Of the twenty-five they were able to locate, ranging in age from five to sixteen, every single one exhibited the rough-and-tumble play more characteristic of boys than girls.

Every single one.

Even at their early age, fourteen of them had already declared themselves to be, in fact, boys—against everything in how they had been raised. From this and scores of other studies, Rhoads concludes that instead of thinking that the difference between the sexes is something learned or imposed by society, it is rather something larger, something deeply rooted in our very nature. It's part of who we are. It's not a role that we take on; it's the very nature of our being.

This isn't about what's known in psychiatry as Gender Identity Disorder. That is something that can be treated. It is about maintaining that gender and sex, in a healthy psychology, are not something simply between our ears but are connected to what's between our legs. Sexuality is not like a favorite color—something to be chosen, or a preference—it is hardwired into our being.

But that is precisely what our culture wishes to ignore.

The Abolition of Man

One of the great questions in all of human thought is, "Who am I?" The answer is fast becoming, "I don't know." It is as though our embrace of plastic surgery has led to a sense of being plastic ourselves, stripped of any sense of innate worth or identity. If human beings have no fixed or permanent essence, if we are "plastic"—subject through technology to alteration, enhancement, mutation, and control—then we may do what we will with ourselves.

And so we have.

It brings to mind the seven-year-old Denver boy who wanted to join the Girl Scouts. Initially rejected on the local level, the state organization revealed the little-known policy that as an "inclusive organization," they were in support of "transgender kids." In a statement on the matter from the Girl Scouts of Colorado, the following was asserted: "We accept all girls in kindergarten through 12th grade as members. If a child identifies as a girl and the child's family presents her as a girl, Girl Scouts of Colorado welcomes her as a Girl Scout."[5]

While the policy has won praise from transgender groups, others are responding to such "inclusion" by calling it nothing less than sexual abuse. Judith A. Reisman, then visiting professor of law at Liberty University School of Law, commented that it is "the violation of children's genetic reality aided by a society that is reverting back to the dark. If he has male parts, he is a male. . . . People used to ask which is stronger, nature or nurture. Now we are so 'smart' we don't even know we have a nature."[6]

Another observer, psychiatrist Keith Ablow, also called it a form of abuse. "This is all [putting] the cart before the horse. We're conducting social, cultural, sexual experiments on the fly, using our own kids as guinea pigs, without the necessary research to guide us."[7]

C. S. Lewis once wrote of the desire to take control over all nature, even human nature, and declare our independence. With full control over ourselves, we will have won the ultimate battle. But what is won? Nothing. This led to Lewis's prediction in a 1947 essay that "Man's final conquest has proved to be the abolition of man."[8]

He seems to have been more prescient than he imagined.

15

The Disappearance of Childhood

American culture is hostile to the idea of childhood.

Neil Postman[1]

Imagine a website that encourages plastic surgery and extreme dieting in the search for the perfect figure. Not hard to imagine, right?

Now imagine such a website designed for girls as young as nine.

Welcome to MissBimbo.com, a website that encourages girls as young as nine to embrace breast implants and face-lifts, along with diet pills for weight loss. In the guise of a virtual reality game, prepubescent girls are encouraged to buy their virtual characters breast enlargement surgery and to keep them "waif thin" with diet pills. Aimed at girls age nine to sixteen, the site attracted 200,000 members during its first month of operation in Britain. The French version of the site boasted 1.2 million players.

The goal of the game is to keep a constant watch on the weight, wardrobe, wealth, and happiness of their character to create "the coolest, richest and most famous bimbo in the world." Participants compete with other children to earn "bimbo dollars" that are then used for plastic surgery, diet pills, face-lifts, lingerie, and fashionable nightclub outfits.

122

Targets are set for users, such as:

Level 7: *After you broke up with your boyfriend you went on an eating binge! Now it's time to diet. . . . Your target weight is less than 132 lbs.*

Level 9: *Have a nip and tuck operation for a brand new face. You've found work as a plus-size model. To gain those vivacious curves, you need to weigh more than 154 lbs.*

Level 10: *Summertime is coming up and bikini weather is upon us. You want to turn heads on the beach, don't you?*

Level 11: *Bigger is better! Have a breast operation.*

Level 17: *There is a billionaire on vacation. . . . You must catch his eye and his love! Good luck!*

According to the *London Times*, healthcare professionals, a parents group, and an organization representing people suffering from anorexia and bulimia criticized the website for sending a dangerous message to impressionable children. Founders of the site admit that "the story in the script for the game had been created by 'lads' and no professional advice was sought about how girls may interpret issues surrounding weight loss and gain." Yet the *Times* also reported that the site was perhaps simply a reflection of an already existing reality, as its introduction came as research showed that children as young as six were developing acute eating disorders such as anorexia and bulimia and increasing numbers of teenagers were undergoing breast enlargement surgery.[2]

Nick Williams from Shrewsbury, England, said that he was appalled when he saw his daughters Katie, age nine, and Sarah, fourteen, on the site pondering whether to buy their character breast operations and face-lifts.

I noticed them looking at possible breast operations and facelifts at the game's plastic surgery clinic. . . . It is irresponsible of the site's creators to be leading young girls astray. They are easily influenced at that age as to what is cool and these are not things they should be encouraged to aspire to before they are old enough to be making up their own minds.[3]

This is far from an isolated case. In what is only the latest in a numbing series of such stories, a new French lingerie line is selling provocative bras and panties for girls ages four through twelve. The catalog for the line, created by Jours Apres Lunes, features child models in full makeup and Lolita-esque poses. The line of lingerie includes bras, panties, and camisoles for toddlers.

Why a four-year-old needs a bra is not explained on the site.[4]

Some Targets from MissBimbo.com

Level 7: *After you broke up with your boyfriend you went on an eating binge! Now it's time to diet. . . . Your target weight is less than 132 lbs.*

Level 9: *Have a nip and tuck operation for a brand new face. You've found work as a plus-size model. To gain those vivacious curves, you need to weigh more than 154 lbs.*

Level 10: *Summertime is coming up and bikini weather is upon us. You want to turn heads on the beach, don't you?*

Level 11: *Bigger is better! Have a breast operation.*

Level 17: *There is a billionaire on vacation . . . You must catch his eye and his love! Good luck!*

Growing Older Younger

Remember "I Am Sixteen, Going on Seventeen" from *The Sound of Music*? Today it would have to be "I Am *Six*, Going on Seventeen."

A new and startling cultural trend is the tendency of children to grow older younger; a trend with its own acronym: G.O.Y. (Growing Older Younger). Pamela Paul's article in the *New York Times* says that this trend has six-year-olds going to school guidance counselors complaining that so-and-so won't play with them because they like the Jonas Brothers and the "it girls" like Miley Cyrus. You see, at six, that's way too juvenile. They should be on to something more age-appropriate, like Lady Gaga.

"It's not cool to not have a cellphone anymore or to not wear exactly the right thing," says Erin Munroe, a school guidance counselor in Boston. "The poor girls who have Strawberry Shortcake shirts on, forget it." Tracy Vaillancourt, who specializes in children's mental health at the University of Ottawa, agrees: "Kids mirror the larger culture, from reality TV to materialism."[5]

But aren't parents actively shielding their children from aspects of culture that are age-inappropriate?

Apparently not.

What seems to be happening is that as select peers grow older younger, the other children feel pressured to match them for the sake of popularity and acceptance. "The girls who are the victims [of bullying or social rejection] tend to be raised by parents who encourage them to be more age appropriate," observes Debbie Rosenman, a teacher in her thirty-first year at a suburban Detroit school. "The mean girls are 8 but want to be 14, and their parents play along."[6]

Soon, wanting their children to fit in, the initially age-appropriate parents start to *give* in, escalating the downward spiral. As author Rosalind Wiseman observes, "Parents think it's really cute when their 2- and 3-year-olds are doing 'Single Ladies' or singing the Alicia Keys/Jay-Z song. But it's not so funny at age 8, when they're singing along to Lady Gaga and demanding a cellphone."[7]

The Disappearance of Childhood

One of sociologist Neil Postman's most provocative works is *The Disappearance of Childhood*. His thesis is that children are being robbed of their innocence, their naiveté, their ability to even *be* a child. He contends that in our world, we ask children to embrace mature issues, themes, and experiences long before they are ready. Postman argues that the very idea of childhood is that it is a time when a young person is sheltered from certain ideas, experiences, practices, expectations, and knowledge. They are sheltered from adult secrets, particularly sexual ones. Certain facets of life—its mysteries, contradictions, tragedies, and violence—are not considered suitable for children to know. Only as a child grows into adulthood are they revealed in ways that they can assimilate psychologically, emotionally, and spiritually.

Postman's analysis, first offered in 1982, was prescient. Today, twelve- and thirteen-year-old girls are among the highest paid models

in America; they are presented to us as knowing and sexually entic-
ing adults. Young adult fiction is as mature in its themes as anything
on the adult lists. The language of adults and children—including
what they address in life—has become the same. It is virtually uncon-
tested among sociologists that the behavior, language, attitudes, and
desires—even the physical appearance—of adults and children are
becoming indistinguishable. And the children on TV act like adults.
They do not differ significantly in their interests, language, dress, or
sexuality from the adults on the show; making the same knowing
wisecracks, and tossing out the same sexual innuendo.

This is why for years the books that were read in the fourth grade or
seventh grade or ninth grade were chosen not only for their vocabulary
and syntax but for content considered to contain fourth, seventh, or
ninth grade information, ideas, and experiences. But when the line
between the adult world and the child's world becomes blurred, or
no longer exists, childhood disappears. And so,

- We let our eight-year-olds watch *Modern Family* or *Glee*.
- We let our girls dress provocatively and begin dating at ridiculously early ages.
- We ignore the fact that our kids have lied to get on Facebook
  (you have to be thirteen), or we have even lied for them so they
  could join.
- While watching the game with our sons, we let GoDaddy.com
  commercials come and go without comment or even changing
  the channel.
- We have no idea what Rhianna, Katy Perry, or Lady Gaga is
  singing to them on their iPod.
- And we don't screen friends.

The Underprotective Parent

There is much talk in our day about avoiding being *overprotective* but
little to no talk on being *underprotective*. It's a significant cultural
question, and it's at the heart of the disappearance of childhood.

Let's go back a few decades. In the 1930s and 40s, parents and
families were conventional, strict, and often focused on appearance.

Then in 1946 came a book titled *Baby and Child Care* by an American pediatrician named Dr. Benjamin Spock. That book continues to shape us today.

Building off the field of psychoanalysis, Dr. Spock told parents to loosen up, back off, and let the child go. They should be more flexible and treat their children as individuals. While he admirably called for love and affection, he often paired that against discipline and control.

Spock's parental guidelines?

- Tell your children they are special, loved, and unique.
- Don't ever spank them.
- Feed them whenever they are hungry.
- Don't try to put them on a schedule.

By 1998 his book had sold more than 50 million copies and had been translated into thirty-nine languages. Many critics feel that the proof of his advice was in the pudding: "What do you get when you raise a generation on the permissive ideas of Dr. Spock, saturate them with rock and roll, introduce them to drugs and alcohol, overshadow them with the threat of nuclear holocaust, and then tell them that God is dead?"

The sixties, replete with LSD, Woodstock, riots in the streets, and free love.

Whether that was a result of new parenting styles or simply the way of the world, the parenting pendulum had swung. From hands on to hands off; from discipline to persuasion; from moral authority to moral influence. And while today we may have backed off from some of the more radical ideas Spock put forward that our parents and their parents embraced, here's what stuck: the one thing you don't want to do as a parent is be overprotective. And we've attached all kinds of pejorative words to it:

- hovering .
- smothering
- babying
- coddling
- sheltering

It sends a very strong message by insinuation: it's wrong to be overprotective, but it's not wrong to be underprotective. If you're going to make a mistake, make a mistake in being loose, in playing fast and free, in not protecting enough. Because the one big parenting sin is protecting too much. This in a world of sexting and Facebook, bullying in schools and internet porn, *Teen Mom* and *Bad Girls Club*, cutting up and hooking up.

Yet we continue to let culture dictate what is normal; if "everyone" is doing it, wearing it, seeing it, going to it, or listening to it, then we feel we will be damaging our child if we don't go along—even though parenting by "everyone" is putting our children's very childhood at risk. Yet some parents are more eager to be liked or accepted by their kids than they are to be *parents* to their kids.

As a result, childhood slowly evaporates. Or as Neil Postman writes, in having access to the previously hidden fruit of adult information, the child is expelled from the garden of childhood.[8]

The Underprotective Parent

From the Teaching Series by James Emery White

Passive Parent

- "What can you do?"
- "You're wearing that? Well, I guess everyone is."
- "You want to watch what? Well, if everyone is."
- "You want to do what? Well, if the others are."

Active Parent

- Informed—knowing what is going on in your children's world; what they are doing, and with whom they are doing it
- Involved—being part of their world; not as a spectator but as a participant
- In charge—leading their world; creating and shaping the context of their life

MP3 and PDF versions available at http://churchandculture.org/media.asp

MEDIA AND TECHNOLOGY

16

Supersaturation

The writer of Ecclesiastes notes that, "Of making many books there
is no end" (Eccles. 12:12). This has been amended several times to
apply to countless endeavors, but perhaps most of all as: "Of making
many *lists* there is no end."

Two recent lists stand out.

First, courtesy of the *Atlantic Monthly*, is a list of the 100 most
influential figures in American history.[2] Beginning with Abraham
Lincoln (no. 1), working down to Herman Melville (no. 100), the
list marks luminaries such as George Washington and Martin Luther
King, Jr., as well as more modern icons such as Walt Disney, Bill
Gates, and Sam Walton.

Far more intriguing, particularly when juxtaposed with the *Atlantic Monthly* list, is that offered by Allan Lazar, Dan Karlan, and
Jeremy Salter, who together compiled a list of the 101 most influential
people who *never* lived.[3] Their idea is how characters of fiction, myth,

legends, television, and movies have shaped our society, changed our behavior, and set the course of history—often more than those who actually existed.

The number one most influential person who never existed? The Marlboro Man.

> *Advertising Age* picked the Marlboro Man as the most powerful brand image of the twentieth century and one of the top advertising campaigns of that era. . . . Marlboro's new image boosted its sales fourfold from 1955 to 1957, and by 1972 it had become the top cigarette brand both in the nation and the world. In 2000 its market share was 35 percent of U.S. cigarette sales, outselling the six next most popular brands *combined*.[4]

For influence, consider the following:

> Between 20 and 30 percent of the U.S. population now smokes. . . . According to the CDC, deaths attributed to smoking total about 440,000 per year in the United States, plus another 9 million serious illnesses (1995–1999).[5]

The authors pose the question, "Why do we start?" and then give the answer:

> Advertising doesn't merely inform us of price and performance, it tells us what products make us successful and attractive . . . [the image of the cowboy was] exactly what adolescents wanted to be—tough, independent, and free of their parents. . . . And thus the Marlboro Man came into existence, not to sell trips to Wyoming but to plant the idea that the right brand of tobacco would give you independence and strength.[6]

So next time you think through what shapes culture, you may want to pass on Ronald Reagan and think Ronald McDonald. And then think about what that particular Ronald is motivating you to become—and more importantly, *how* he is doing it.

There is little doubt about the intentionality of the media to shape and form, influence and lead. For example, think of MTV. Martha Quinn, one of the five original MTV "VJs," reflects, "We were rebels with a cause, and we had the rock 'n' roll generation and the television

> ## The Top 10 of the 100
> ## Most Influential Figures in American History
> Atlantic Monthly
>
> 1. Abraham Lincoln (1809–1865)
> 2. George Washington (1732–1799)
> 3. Thomas Jefferson (1743–1826)
> 4. Franklin Delano Roosevelt (1882–1945)
> 5. Alexander Hamilton (1755–1804)
> 6. Benjamin Franklin (1706–1790)
> 7. John Marshall (1755–1835)
> 8. Martin Luther King, Jr. (1929–1968)
> 9. Thomas Edison (1847–1931)
> 10. Woodrow Wilson (1856–1924)

generation behind us." Now, with around 100 channels and over a billion viewers, MTV does not reflect youth culture—it creates it. Or as MTV's founding chairman Bob Pittman stated in a 1982 interview, "If you can get their emotions going, make them forget their logic, you've got them. At MTV, we don't shoot for the 14-year-olds, we own them."

And nowhere does media own us more than in regard to our sexual lives.

As mentioned in an earlier chapter, studies show that most children are exposed to sexual content three times more often on television shows than on the internet, with music also a much greater influence than the Web.

And it's quite an exposure.

Consider the television show *Friends*, which ran for ten years between 1994 and 2004. A survey of all 236 episodes of the NBC sitcom found that the characters had a total of eighty-five sexual partners (counting only those who appeared on-screen).[7]

Fred Fedler, author of one of the most widely used college textbooks on the mass media, writes that "the media may constitute the most powerful education system ever known to man."[8] Supporting this contention, the Public Agenda Poll, conducted by the Nickelodeon

The Top 10 of the 101 Most Influential People Who *Never* Lived

1. The Marlboro Man
2. Big Brother
3. King Arthur
4. Santa Claus
5. Hamlet
6. Dr. Frankenstein's Monster
7. Siegfried
8. Sherlock Holmes
9. Romeo and Juliet
10. Dr. Jekyll and Mr. Hyde

cable network and a marketing and social research firm, found that today, children get more of their information about all of life—not just sex—from TV than they do from their parents.[9]

Media presentations are wildly biased, and often openly so, and in ways that go far beyond the liberal bent of MSNBC or the conservative tilt of Fox.[10] There are foundational issues related to worldview and selection of what is true. The significance is not simply the exposure to such perspectives but rather our tendency to never question them. Film director Oliver Stone—deflecting criticism for the distortions and factual errors in his films, particularly the feigned documentary exposé on the Kennedy assassination, *JFK*—once said in a lecture at American University that films shouldn't be the end-all for what is true. "[People] have a responsibility to read a book," he said. "[Nobody] is going to sit through a three-hour movie and say, 'That's that.'"[11]

He's wrong. That is exactly what they do.

Further, this onslaught is largely devoid of meaning. "What we've introduced with MTV," says Bob Pittman, "is a nonnarrative form. . . . We rely on *mood* and *emotion*. We make you feel a certain way as opposed to you walking away with any particular knowledge."[12]

Immersion

The average child between the age of eight to eighteen "now spends practically every waking minute—except for the time in school—using a smart phone, computer, television or other electronic device," according to a study that didn't receive the wide discussion it deserved when released in 2010 by the Kaiser Family Foundation. Specifically, they spend more than seven and a half hours a day with such devices. And that doesn't count the one and a half hours spent texting or the half hour they talk on their cell phones. Because they multitask (for example, surfing the net while listening to their iPod), they manage to cram nearly eleven hours of media content into that seven and a half hours.[13]

In the *Matrix* films, the matrix is an artificial world created by computers in order to immerse human minds into a false reality to keep them subdued. Their true lives are carried out in isolated containers for the harvesting of their bodily energy. But the matrix is so complete, so all-encompassing, that it keeps the mind at bay and in full submission.

The media is *our* matrix. It is not that the communications we live with deceive, broadcast a limiting ideology, emphasize sex and violence, convey diminished images of the good, the true, and the normal, corrode the quality of art, or reduce language—all of which they do. It is that they saturate our lives with the promise of meaning. Todd Gitlin concludes that "the torrent of images, songs, and stories streaming has become our familiar world." Playing off Marshall McLuhan's famous phrase, "the medium is the message," Gitlin suggests that the "montage is the message."[14]

Media Torrent

Gitlin calls this new supersaturation of the media the "media torrent."[15] This torrent determines what we see, and what we don't; what we think about, and what never enters our mind. "All media work us over completely," Marshall McLuhan warns. "They are so pervasive in their personal, political, economic, aesthetic, psychological, moral, ethical, and social consequences that they leave no part of us untouched, unaffected, unaltered."[16]

And most of the time, we fail to see our immersion.

Gitlin offers a parable about a customs officer who observes a truck pulling up at the border. Suspicious, he conducts a thorough and painstaking search of the vehicle but finds nothing. This begins a pattern in which week by week the driver approaches the border, the truck is searched, but nothing is found. Yet the customs officer is convinced that there is contraband. Finally after many years, the officer is set to retire. Once again, the driver pulls up, and the officer says, "I know you're a smuggler. . . . Don't bother denying it. But . . . [I can't] figure out what you've been smuggling all these years. I'm leaving now. I swear to you I can do you no harm. Won't you please tell me what you've been smuggling?"

"Trucks," the driver says.

Gitlin's suggestion is that the media has been smuggling *the habit of living with the media*. What is most at hand, Gitlin argues, is the "experience of media, the sheer quantity of attention paid." Further, the attraction is "satisfaction, the feeling of feelings." It promises "life right now."[17]

Findings from the Kaiser Family Foundation's Research on Children and Technology

- The average child between the ages of eight and eighteen spends nearly every waking minute using a smart phone, computer, television, or other electronic device
- Children spend more than seven and a half hours per day with such devices
- With multitasking (e.g., listening to their iPod while surfing the internet) they cram eleven hours of media content into the seven and a half hours

---

Our changing sense of reality is due, in large part, to reality becoming the torrent of media—and understanding reality in and through that torrent. Since the media do little else but present perspective, the immersion is complete. By conveying to us that everything is a matter of personal perspective, the media torrent has itself become the dominant perspective, exercising the most complete will to power of all.

Yet despite the alarming amount of time being spent with media and the negatives associated with its heavy use, many in cultural leadership encourage the torrent's acceptance. Dr. Michael Rich, a pediatrician at Children's Hospital Boston who directs the Center on Media and Child Health, has said that it is time to stop arguing over whether it is good or bad and accept it as part of children's environment.[18]

In other words, accept the matrix as reality.

17

Homo Interneticus

The medium is the message.
Marshall McLuhan

We like email.

In 2007, 35 trillion email messages shot back and forth between the world's 1 billion PCs; in the time it took you to read that fact, another 300 million emails have been sent and received. It is estimated that in 2009 the average corporate worker spent more than 40 percent of his or her day sending and receiving about two hundred messages.[1]

We also like social media.

Facebook had 1 trillion page views, with over 870 million unique visitors, in June of 2011. Not *by* June 2011, but *in* June 2011.[2] According to the Pew Internet and American Life Project, half of all American adults are now on social networks.[3]

But what we really like is what makes it all possible: the internet. Internet users in the United States jumped from just over 22 million in 2000 to over 245 million in 2010.[4] There can be little doubt that the defining mark of the new generation is that it has never known life without the internet. As Don Tapscott writes, children are "growing up digital."[5]

When Steve Jobs announced the original iPhone as little more than a combination of three revolutionary projects—a cell phone, an iPod, and a handheld computer with internet connectivity and no keyboard—even he didn't know what had been unleashed. Beyond the over 400,000 applications and counting, it opened the door to what Brian Chen calls the "anything-anytime-anywhere future" where we are constantly connected to a global internet community via handheld, incredibly capable gadgets with ubiquitous access to data. As he titles his book, we now live in a world that is "always on."[6] Barnaby Lenon, chairman of the Independent Schools Council in the U.K., has gone so far as to say that even children are becoming addicted to computer use.[7]

But the way the internet is changing our world—and ourselves—runs deeper than that. As Lee Siegel notes, we now "shop, play, work, love, search for information, seek to communicate with each other and sometimes with the world online."[8] The Net Generation does life differently than any other generation; the way they think, learn, play, interact, communicate, purchase, build wealth, create . . . it's all *different* from the way previous generations went about the same tasks.

What does this mean?

How We Think

A fascinating study was conducted by Stanford professor Clifford Nass in 2009 in order to determine the effects of media multitasking on concentration. Those who engaged in heavy multitasking, courtesy of the internet, were less able to focus on a single task.[9]

An earlier study was conducted in 2007 at UCLA. The goal was to study the internet's effect on brain activity. Volunteers wore goggles that projected webpages while submitting to a whole-brain magnetic resonance image. Novices to Web surfing, after only six days of one hour of surfing each day, began showing dramatic changes in brain activity. Gary Small, a professor at UCLA, concluded that the internet is "rapidly and profoundly altering our brains." Pulling from the Stanford and UCLA studies, Nicholas Carr drew a startling conclusion in his book *The Shallows: What the Internet Is Doing to Our Brain*: the internet is weakening our comprehension and transforming us into shallow thinkers.[10]

Tim Challies writes that it is a simple and inevitable progression: "With the ever-present distractions in our lives, we are quickly becoming a people of shallow thoughts, and shallow thoughts will lead to shallow living."[11] Anecdotally, it seems to be an ongoing descent—the more we use the internet, the worse it gets. Though millions of websites exist, along with countless pages of books chronicling the knowledge of millennia, we seem more dependent than ever on news and information sound bites from Yahoo or AOL. The most energy we seem willing to expend is a quick search on Google. Or as Challies writes, "We have become scanners rather than engagers, skimmers in place of readers."[12] It brings to mind something the late historian Daniel Boorstin once suggested: "The greatest menace to progress is not ignorance, but the illusion of knowledge."[13]

But it is not simply our minds that are being transformed; it is also the very nature of our relational world.

Did You Know?

- In 2007, 35 trillion messages shot back and forth between the world's 1 billion PCs.
- In 2011, 160 billion emails were sent daily.
- In the time it took you to read that fact, about 300 million more emails were sent and received.

On but Alone

The heart of the change to our relational lives is simple: "We spend more time alone than ever before."[14]

And apparently, more time doing nothing.

Studies show that for people under the age of thirty, the Web is mostly a time killer. On any given day, 53 percent of all the young adults ages eighteen to twenty-nine go online for no particular reason except to have fun or pass the time.[15]

So what is isolation and waste doing to us?

More than you may imagine.

Ways of Relating

As Maggie Jackson titled one of her books on the matter, we are *distracted*. *Relationally* distracted. Her lament is simple: How did we get to the point where we keep one eye on our Blackberry and one eye on our spouse—in bed? How did we get to the point where we tweet on vacation, text during family dinners, read e-mails during meetings and classes, and learn about our spouse's day on Facebook?

Of course how we got to this point may not be as important as what it is doing to us. Jackson's conclusion is direct: "The way we live is eroding our capacity for deep, sustained, perceptive attention—the building block of intimacy, wisdom, and cultural progress."[16] Studies bear out her concern. According to the psychological research of Larry Rosen of California State University, teens who spend an abundance of time on social networks like Facebook are more likely to show narcissistic tendencies and display signs of other behavioral problems.[17] Specifically, they become more prone to vain, aggressive, antisocial behavior. It's certainly giving rise to new forms of harassment, from cyber-stalking to cyber-bullying.

As mentioned in an earlier chapter, the 2010 Kaiser Family Foundation study also found that heavy media use, amplified and energized by the internet, is associated with behavior problems, poor grades, and obesity. According to the study, the "heaviest media users were also more likely to report that they were bored or sad, or that they got into trouble, did not get along well with their parents and were not happy at school."[18]

Perhaps one of the more intriguing studies related to the way the internet affects our behavior researched the relationship between texting and lying. A study published in 2012 in the *Journal of Business Ethics* found that people are more likely to lie via text than any other form of communication, such as when compared to face-to-face communications, video conferencing, or audio chat. The researchers say that lying via text makes intuitive sense because it is known as *lean media*, which means it doesn't convey the important emotional cues that signal someone may be lying—such as stuttering, twisting your hands nervously, or darting your eyes. When lying is covered up by lean media, it opens the door of temptation to lie even more.[19]

So it isn't simply that the new media are changing how we do life, they are changing the very character of our lives. We do not simply text each other; who we are to each other changes *because* we text.

Pop Quiz

Heavy media use in children is associated with which of the following issues:

   a. behavior problems
   b. poor grades
   c. obesity
   d. boredom or depression
   e. poor relationship with parents
   f. unhappiness at school
   g. all of the above

The right answer: g.

Lack of Civility

Being isolated also affects civility. For the first time, any individual can—with anonymity—establish a media platform from which to not only publicize and promote but also demonize and denounce.

A recent editorial in *Christianity Today* discussed how no attribute of civilized life seems more under attack than civility. The author, David Aikman, noted the extent to which certain Christians have turned themselves into the "self-appointed attack dogs of Christendom."

> They seem determined to savage not only opponents of Christianity, but also fellow believers of whose doctrinal positions they disapprove. A troll through the Internet reveals websites so drenched in sarcasm and animosity that an agnostic, or a follower of another faith tradition interested in what it means to become a Christian, might be permanently disillusioned.[20]

I read of a large church that made the news due to a problem with a persistently caustic blogger. A former member, he had become disgruntled over various actions of the senior pastor, and he became further incensed that said pastor maintained the backing of the leadership. With nowhere to go with his animus, and no means to lobby for his cause, he started an anonymous blog in order to wage a one-person campaign of bitterness. It quickly disintegrated on both sides to such a degree that the church complained to the police, who investigated and discovered the identity of the blogger, and now suits and countersuits are flying freely.

What a God-forsaken mess.

As I researched the article, I found it had links that led to other links, and before I knew it, I found myself exposed in a way I had never imagined possible to the sordid world of the bitter-blog—which means blogs that seem to exist for no other reason than to attack (or at least pick apart) a particular Christian leader, church, or ministry. I found that virtually every senior pastor of a celebrity megachurch is the subject of a bitter-blog that is intent on causing dissension, disunity, and as much disaffection as possible.

This is a new and explosive development. Anyone with an axe to grind or a grudge to nurse can launch a website for global consumption. It can be done with complete anonymity, virtually no cost, and most important of all, no accountability or consequences. This shouldn't be underestimated. While personal disagreements have always plagued the human community, much was worked out by necessity. We still had to see that person, even depend on him or her to function in society. Now, with the internet, it is as though we can pillory at will.

Our Sense of Self

Not only has the internet altered our sense of community, but it has even redefined our sense of self-worth. We tend to evaluate ourselves by how many fans we have on Facebook, how many followers we have on Twitter, and how much traffic we have for our blog. It is as though a new layer has been built between us and others—a new area that demonstrates our worth and standing. There is no longer just me and you and our families, schools, sports, or arts. There is now an online identity and presence that is as decisive to our sense of well-being as clothes, appearance, and wealth. This has become such a part of children's lives that the American Academy of Pediatrics is urging pediatricians to make asking about media usage a standard part of checkups. Experts are even coining the phrase "Facebook depression" to describe the low self-esteem kids can experience from constant exposure to friends' happy status updates and photos of someone else's packed social calendar.

Homo Interneticus

In the past we have called ourselves a race of *Homo sapiens*, which means "thinking beings." Lee Siegel suggests that perhaps we should consider a new name: *Homo interneticus*.[21] Our primary identity is quickly becoming *connected* beings. When Marshall McLuhan coined the phrase, "The medium is the message," his point was that the way we gain our information shapes us more than the information itself.

McLuhan was right.

18

New News

The revolution will be twitterised.

Dominic Rushe[1]

It's a new day for news.

Newspapers face declining circulation; old-guard magazines, such as *Newsweek*, teeter on the brink of extinction; and icons of the traditional press, such as Howard Fineman of *Newsweek*, Peter Goodman of the *New York Times*, and Howard Kurtz of the *Washington Post*, are jumping to such digital media upstarts as the *Huffington Post* and the *Daily Beast*.

But it's not simply a day when the old forms of journalism are struggling. It's a day when new forms of communication are taking their place.

Sometimes with nothing more than a tweet.

News in 140 Characters

It's time to state the obvious: with over 100 million active users sending more than 5 billion tweets a month, Twitter has become the people's voice.[2] To put the growth of Twitter in perspective, in June of 2010 there were 65 million tweets being sent per day. By September of 2011 that number had jumped to 230 million.[3]

As Dominic Rushe wrote in the *Guardian*, "Twitter is part of a social media revolution that is reordering the way the world communicates, shaking up politics, business and social life and even, some argue, fueling and coordinating historic upheavals from Iran and Tunisia to Egypt. The revolution will be twitterised."[4] Twitter is "the first people's broadcast medium," observes author and media theorist Douglas Rushkoff. "You can do it now, it can go everywhere, and you don't have to sit with it. The best thing about Twitter is that it is not sticky the way things like Facebook are. I can throw out tweets without having to field a zillion emails or nurse some profile or deal with anything else. I can fling and not receive." Or as Paul Kedrosky, twitterholic investor and author of the "Infectious Greed" blog, says, the service has become the "ubiquitous fabric" of online real-time conversation. "Twitter is the dial tone," he says. "It's transforming how we communicate."[5]

In the social media universe, Facebook continues to be the all-purpose hub for posting everything social. Blogs continue to be the home for more substantive conversations. But Twitter is becoming the way we spread news, offer comment or feedback, disseminate updates, and even direct larger audiences to other social media platforms.

For many observers, 2011 was the year Twitter came of age in terms of news. From the Arab Spring to the Royal Wedding, the sudden death of Kim Jong Il to the rescue of the Chilean miners, Twitter led the way in breaking news. Consider the capture and killing of Osama Bin Laden. In May 2011, little did IT consultant Sohaib Athar know that when he tweeted, "Helicopter hovering above Abbottabad at 1AM (is a rare event)," he was witnessing something more significant than he could have imagined. As he later tweeted, "Uh oh, now I'm the guy who liveblogged the Osama raid without knowing it."[6]

And in many ways, that is the downside. Tweets are spontaneous, quick and unvetted. We have the power of the tweet, but we seldom pause long enough to wonder whether what we are about to say should be tweeted. "Facebook and Twitter do not encourage this kind of self-restraint. In fact, they encourage an opposing value system," John Dyer observes. "Social media relentlessly asks us to publish our personal opinions on anything and everything that happens. There is no time for reflection in prayer, no place for discussion with other flesh and blood image bearers, and no incentive to remain silent."[7]

So with the tweet, the news is immediate, but so immediate that it is difficult to discuss how newsworthy—much less accurate—it is.

A Bias toward Bias

There is much to be applauded in this new world. News can "land hard no matter the platform," and with astonishing immediacy, writes David Carr of the *New York Times*. "The speed with which a media brand can be built—see Huffington Post for the most breathtaking example—means that the barriers to entry that made the media business the province of titans are gone." But Carr also reveals some dangerous trends in our embrace of the new news. While on a journalistic level the playing field is more even, many people see the news "in aggregated form on the Web, and when they notice a link that interests them, they click on it with nary a thought about the news organization behind it. Information stands or falls on its magnetism."

The Importance of Fact-Checking

September 8, 2004—Dan Rather, on *60 Minutes*, presented four documents critical of President George W. Bush's service in the Texas Air National Guard. It was later discovered that CBS and Rather did not take the time to authenticate the documents, which turned out to be forgeries.

October 15, 2009—Richard and Mayumi Heene claimed their six-year-old son Falcon was floating away in a large gas balloon, launching a media frenzy, the closing of the Denver airport, and the mobilization of National Guard helicopters and local police in pursuit. All of it was a hoax perpetrated by the parents to gain media attention.

August 30, 2010—Bethany Storro claimed she was attacked outside a Starbucks in downtown Vancouver and had acid thrown on her face. This moved the community to start a relief fund to help her, only to find out that it was a hoax.

Carr continues, "More and more, media outlets are becoming a federation of individual brands." In this way, "Journalism is starting to look like sports, where a cast of role players serves as a platform and context for highly paid, high-impact players."[8] To carry the sports motif forward, each of these teams has its own identity. Any attempt at neutrality is, at best, thinly veiled. You can't watch the *Today Show* on NBC and not experience the liberal bias of the hosts in maddening ways. The same can be said of the conservative tilt at Fox.

Going further, open Gawker, CNN, NPR, and the *Wall Street Journal* on your iPad and see if you can tell without looking at the name which is a blog, a television brand, a radio network, or a newspaper. As Carr notes, they all have text, links, video, and pictures. News, it seems, is wherever the public finds it. And whatever the media outlet wants it to be.

Also, the immediacy of news means that there is less feedback, fact-checking, copy-checking, and double-checking. In other words, all news now stands at a greater risk of being not only misleading but inaccurate. Remember "balloon boy"? The girl attacked with acid? The report of memos critical of George W. Bush's Texas Air National Guard service record made public by Dan Rather but later found to be forgeries?

There is also a greater tendency to associate news stories with specific agendas. Not simply bias, but agenda. For example, a homosexual man at Rutgers hanged himself when a videotape of him having sex with another man was broadcast on the internet. In close proximity of time, a gay man in the Bronx was beaten because he was gay. These stories were both sad and horrific. But they were quickly associated with anyone who condemned homosexuality, as if taking any such moral stand was akin to inciting further hate crimes. This was, of course, a ridiculous connection that seemed intent on taking advantage of a sensational news cycle to silence anyone speaking out against homosexuality as a morally acceptable lifestyle.

But such intentions are now commonplace.

As a result, gaining discernment in regard to the news has never been more pressing. Howard K. Smith, a news icon in the golden age of television news in the 1960s and 1970s, once quipped that the media may not tell you what to think, but they most certainly tell you what to think about.

Now even that demarcation is extinct.

Through the bias of the author, the choice of interviewees, the selection of questions, the camera angle, and the power of editing, we are told what to think, what to think *about*, and how to feel—all with little sense of knowing how to determine what is actually true.

One Saint or Two?

One of the most vivid examples of the media's power to set such an agenda came to my attention on a September morning in 1997 while I was doing my morning run at the gym. There is a bank of televisions in front of the treadmills, and on this particular morning I watched the entire *CNN Headline News* program from 8:30 to 9:00 a.m.[9] The first fifteen minutes were spent on Princess Diana, who had been killed a week earlier in a car crash. There was a story on her funeral. Then came a story on how her boys would handle her death and the media scrutiny that would now surely follow their lives. Then came a report on the song that Elton John had composed for her funeral, followed by footage of the bells pealing throughout England for her death. Then came another story on the eulogies that had been given at her burial. Only two other events, Hurricane Erica and the Space Station *Mir*, received coverage during the news segment of the program. When these two additional stories were completed, the newscast went back to Elton John singing his new version of "Candle in the Wind."

That was it.

CNN then went right into its business news, its sports segment, and then its entertainment/lifestyle coverage. Considering that at the time CNN was America's leading cable news network, you would think it was just a slow news day. Or that the death of Princess Diana was such a monumental event that it deserved to dominate the newscast. Yet I knew that something *else* had happened the night before, something that was never mentioned—*not even once*. There was another death to take note of. A small, old Albanian woman named Agnes had passed away—better known to the world as Mother Teresa. Newsworthy? To say the least. Mother Teresa was a Nobel Prize winner and arguably the most beloved woman in the entire world.

But she was never even mentioned.

CNN wasn't alone. According to the Media Research Center, the ratio of coverage of Diana to Mother Teresa on the CBS Evening News ran 3 to 1 and on NBC, 7 to 1. *Newsweek* magazine had forty-seven pages on Diana, but only four on Mother Teresa. *Time* and *U.S. News and World Report* weren't much better.[10]

However, it wasn't just the extent of the coverage but the way it was covered. Andrew Morton, as part of an ABC news story, said that Diana's death was "one of the most awful tragedies of the late twentieth century, if not the greatest. In her death something inside us had died. People are grieving for lost hopes, lost dreams, lost ambitions."[11]

That's a very emotional assessment. And then, when coupled with constant scenes of grief and crying, we were led to feel that this was a loss of cosmic proportions. Now, nothing against Diana, but not only was her death nowhere near the greatest tragedy that had occurred to the world over the previous fifty years leading up to her death—eclipsing such things as Vietnam, Chernobyl, Tiananmen Square, or the explosion of the space shuttle *Challenger*—but even when compared to the loss of other figures such as Mother Teresa, she lived a life of very little significance. As one person quipped, she was just famous for being famous. She actually did very little. But the media led us to feel that her life greatly overshadowed Mother Teresa's.

So much so that the talk was not that Mother Teresa would be made a saint, but that Princess Di would.

The Daily Me

Perhaps the greatest temptation of the *new* news is its personalization. Now we are able to filter out any information we do not wish to consider. This creates what University of Chicago professor Cass Sunstein has called the "Daily Me" —a self-created world in which we see only the sports highlights that concern our favorite team, read only the issues that address our interests, and engage only the op-ed pieces with which we agree.[12] The highly lauded personalization of information protects us from exposure to anything that may challenge our thinking or make us uncomfortable.

The "Daily Me" solidifies divisions between such things as political or religious sides, giving greater identity to ideological persuasions. So we don't listen to something such as National Public Radio for news; we listen to hear our personal beliefs affirmed. If our beliefs are challenged, we complain or simply change stations.

So unchecked, we begin to follow the sound of nothing more than the echo of our own voice.

19

Is Google God?

When we know it, you'll know it.

CNN

Is Google God?

Columnist Thomas Friedman posed this question in his article by that name in the *New York Times* in June of 2003. Quoting the vice president of a Wi-Fi provider, Friedman writes that "Google, combined with Wi-Fi, is a little bit like God. God is wireless, God is everywhere and God sees and knows everything. Throughout history, people connected to God without wires. Now, for many questions in the world, you ask Google, and increasingly, you can do it without wires, too."[1]

Now Friedman's question seems prescient. Taken from *googol* (the numeral 1 followed by 100 zeros), signifying how much information Google initially hoped to catalog, *googling* has now become synonymous with the search for information. Following its lucrative initial public offering, Google announced arrangements with the New York Public Library, along with the libraries of Harvard University, Stanford University, the University of Oxford, and the University of Michigan to digitize virtually every holding. It is as if the internet was made for Google.

Interestingly, when the Web's inventor, Tim Berners-Lee, first imagined it, he named it "Enquire," short for *Enquire Within upon Everything*, a "musty old book of Victorian advice I noticed as a child in my parents' house outside London. With its title suggestive of magic, the book served as a portal to a world of information, everything from how to remove clothing stains to tips on investing money."[2]

His original title was more prophetic than he could have imagined.

There can be little doubt that what began as a graduate project of two twentysomething Stanford students—Google—is now shaping the world. But how? Few would deny the convenience of the project and the value it can bring, but there are troubling dynamics. One in particular: the trivialization of knowledge.

As laudable as the library project may be, among the most popular Google searches of 2010 were Justin Bieber and Lady Gaga. In 2011 the top ten included YouTube phenom Rebecca Black and the game Battlefield 3.[3] Because of the internet, there is a widening chasm between wisdom and information. Quentin Schultze writes that the torrent of information now at our disposal is often little more than "endless volleys of nonsense, folly, and rumor masquerading as knowledge, wisdom, and even truth."[4]

Chuck Kelley, president of New Orleans Baptist Theological Seminary, recently noted that "Google has changed the relationship of people to information. For the last 300 or 400 years, information has been collected on college, university and seminary campuses. . . . You went to the collected information to learn. Today the information is available anywhere you want, just Google it."[5]

This creates a new challenge for educators. Rather than primarily dispensing information, Kelley said educators must spend much more of their time helping students *evaluate* information. He's right. It is as though we've dropped a library card onto the world but removed the classroom that gives us the literacy to read its contents, much less the education needed to interpret its contents.

For example, do a Google search for "Easter." At the time of this writing, you will get 240,000,000 results. One of the top responses on the first page of hits is from www.religioustolerance.org, headlined on Google as "Easter: Its Origins and Meanings." Sounds promising. But then you read the following:

Modern-day Easter is derived from two ancient traditions: one Judeo-Christian and the other Pagan. Both Christians and Pagans have celebrated death and resurrection themes following the Spring Equinox for millennia. Most religious historians believe that many elements of the Christian observance of Easter were derived from earlier Pagan celebrations.[6]

Um, no.

As historian Anthony McRoy counters:

The argument largely rests on the supposed pagan associations of the English and German *names* for the celebration (*Easter* in English and *Ostern* in German). It is important to note, however, that in most other European languages, the name for the Christian celebration is derived from the Greek word *Pascha*, which comes from *pesach*, the Hebrew word for Passover. Easter is the Christian Passover festival.

Of course, even if Christians did engage in contextualization—expressing their message and worship in the language or forms of the local people—that in no way implies doctrinal compromise. Christians around the world have sought to redeem the local culture for Christ while purging it of practices antithetical to biblical norms. After all, Christians speak of "Good Friday," but they are in no way honoring the worship of the Norse/Germanic queen of the gods Freya (which gives us the word "Friday") by doing so.

But, in fact, in the case of Easter the evidence suggests otherwise: that neither the commemoration of Christ's death and resurrection nor its name are derived from paganism.[7]

McRoy is a Fellow of the British Society for Middle East Studies and a lecturer in Islamic studies. In other words, he is a leading scholar in this field. The author of the Google article? At first glance, unnamed. Dig deeper into the site's basement and you find it is sponsored by the "Ontario Consultants on Religious Tolerance." Dig even deeper and you find that almost all of the more than 4,000 essays and menus on this website were written by its main author and coordinator, Bruce A. Robinson.[8] He is a graduate of the University of Toronto, class of 1959, with a BaSc (Bachelor of Applied Science) degree in engineering physics and no other advanced degrees, much less a degree in history. You also find that he is a member of the Unitarian Universalist Church and calls himself an agnostic.

Which googled article will people tend to read and believe? Obviously the one delivered most readily by Google. In the case of Easter, this would mean false and terribly misleading information on the most critical of events involving the life of Christ.

And that is the problem.

The more dependent we are on specific technological portals for information, and the less educated we are to discern the value of where those portals lead us, the more captive we will be to that source of knowledge and that source alone.

The great Solomon had a defining moment with just this issue:

> Now, LORD my God, you have made your servant king in place of my father David. But I am only a little child and do not know how to carry out my duties. Your servant is here among the people you have chosen, a great people, too numerous to count or number. So give your servant a discerning heart to govern your people and to distinguish between right and wrong. For who is able to govern this great people of yours?
>
> 1 Kings 3:7–9

It is precisely the disconnect between what is right and what is wrong that makes wisdom so indispensable and more information, apart from wisdom, so dangerous.

And wisdom can't be googled.

But the larger cultural current is how technology has become our god, and its providers our spiritual guides. Nothing brought this into the light of day more than a single death.

A Most Curious Hero

This man is a hero to many:

- His father is Abdulfattah Jandali, a Syrian Muslim.
- He denied the paternity of his first child, claiming he was sterile, leaving the mother to raise his daughter on welfare checks.
- There is no record that he ever gave any money to charity, and when he became CEO of his company, he stopped all of their philanthropic programs as well.

- In order to increase his own financial gain, he lied to the co-founder of his company about the amount of money they were to receive for a project because it was to be split fifty-fifty.
- He was a Zen Buddhist, and he and his wife were married by his guru, a Zen monk.
- He went to college for one semester and then dropped out.
- He used LSD and even called it "one of the two or three most important things I have done in my life."[9]

His name? Steve Jobs, former CEO of Apple, whose early death from pancreatic cancer reverberated around the world as one of the great tragedies of the modern era. The depth of mourning was staggering, yet the only tie most had with him was the iPad by which they received the news.

I stand in awe of his creative genius as much as anyone. I was saddened by his many health challenges. But my point is simple: what a curious hero. What elevated Jobs to the role of secular spiritual guru? It seems only one thing: our cultural fascination—yes, even worship—of technology. Steve Jobs was heralded because he invented the Mac, the iPod, the iPhone, and the iPad. We so cherish those technological achievements that we award honor and even moral stature to their creator.

No doubt, the technology from Jobs has been amazing. No creator has shaped culture as much through invention since Edison; no CEO has shaped culture as much through production since Henry Ford and his Model T.

But unlike those before him, with his technological prowess came the status of spiritual icon.

Here was the god who brought fire down from the sky.

20

Celebrification

Life has become a show staged for the media.

Neal Gabler[1]

What would you do for fame?

I know, the reality TV phenomenon should already have answered that for us. But really, what would you be willing to do? Just fill in the blank:

I am willing to do _____for fame.

For one aspiring actress, the answer is "porn."

Her name is Montana Fishburne. And yes, she is the daughter of *that* Fishburne—the Oscar-nominated actor Laurence Fishburne. "My dad is very upset" and "very hurt," she acknowledged. Yet as DeWayne Wickham reports in *USA Today*, she is bound and determined to follow through on her plan to "become a Hollywood A-lister by launching her film career among the industry's bottom feeders."[2]

To her credit, she has seen this work for both Paris Hilton and Kim Kardashian. Both of them were catapulted to notoriety and opportunity by the release of homemade sex tapes. So perhaps we shouldn't be shocked by her line of thinking. "I'm impatient about getting well-known and hav[ing] more opportunities," said the daughter of the acting legend, "and this seemed like a great way to get started on it."[3]

She's not alone. A CNN/Time poll conducted in June of 2000 found that 31 percent of all respondents would be willing to allow a reality show to film them in their pajamas, 29 percent kissing, 26 percent crying, 25 percent having an argument with someone, 16 percent drunk, 10 percent eating a rat or insect, 8 percent naked, and 5 percent having sex.[4]

Lifestyles of the Rich and Famous

Perhaps the actual year 1984 was more Orwellian than we realized, for it was the year *Lifestyles of the Rich and Famous* first aired on American TV. As Robert Thompson, director of the Center for the Study of Popular Television at Syracuse University, noted, "*Lifestyles of the Rich and Famous* marked the beginning of the television obsession with celebrity lifestyle. The show simply gushed. It was all *Isn't this just so wonderful and wouldn't you love to eat off these gold plates, and drink from these diamond-studded goblets, and go to these parties, and live in these houses?* And the formula worked, because it allowed us to imagine ourselves in their shoes."[5] Thompson notes that before World War II, a person living in a small town could go days without seeing the image of a single celebrity, whereas today it's doubtful that the same person in the same town could pass a single day without a glimpse of several.

Lifestyles was soon eclipsed by *American Idol*, the ultimate competition for fame. Suddenly the exposure to celebrity was matched with the opportunity to become one. Add in the explosion of reality TV, and suddenly everyone from pregnant teens to "real" housewives became household names. An article in the *Dallas Morning News* titled "Living in a *People* Magazine Culture," noted that reality TV stars "are like lottery winners, ordinary people spontaneously made extraordinary."[6]

It's Friday

Every year Google sorts through billions of searches to capture that year's fastest-rising global queries. For 2011 it was not the iPhone or Steve Jobs, the earthquake in Japan or the upcoming presidential elections.

It was a thirteen-year-old girl named Rebecca Black.[7]

Unless you were sleeping under a rock that year, you know about the internet sensation surrounding her video "Friday." There were many angles:

- her age—thirteen
- the video—her parents paid to have the song written and the video made for YouTube
- her singing—her voice . . . um . . . needs time to reach its full potential
- the lyrics—if there were an award for the most inane in the world, it would win
- the tune—annoyingly infectious
- the number of hits—before taken off of YouTube, it was at 95,000,000 and climbing
- the harsh, even cruel criticism of the online comments

But the main story is how she reflects the new democratization of media, giving anyone and everyone access to the mass market and, as a result, pseudo-celebrity status.

And it's not just with music. Writers no longer have to work with publishers; Amazon and Kindle can offer their work directly to readers. Almost anyone can develop an app and sell it online.

And the cost? Minimal, if anything. Black's parents paid a reported $2,000 for her video-song package. Result? Nearly 100 million views. A blogger can start for virtually nothing and soon have a following exceeding a syndicated columnist. Apps can be developed with relative ease and little cost.

The positive side is self-evident. No longer does a media elite determine who gets heard, read, or considered.

And the dark side?

Interestingly, the same thing. Anyone and everyone has access to the mass market, which makes the allure of celebrity all that much greater—anyone truly can access it.

How Much Would You Be Willing to Do on a Reality Show?

Results from a CNN/TIME Magazine Poll

- 31 percent would be filmed in their pajamas
- 29 percent would be filmed kissing
- 26 percent would be filmed crying
- 25 percent would be filmed having an argument
- 16 percent would be filmed drunk
- 10 percent would be filmed eating a rat or insect
- 8 percent would be filmed naked
- 5 percent would be filmed having sex

New American Heroes

It's not surprising that our obsession with celebrity is reflected in the shift in American heroes. Since 1946 the Gallup organization has been polling and ranking the most admired Americans. In 1963 that list included such names as Lyndon Johnson, Winston Churchill, Charles de Gaulle, and Martin Luther King, Jr.

Not a single "celebrity" made the list.

Fast forward to the 2011 compilation. Now we have Oprah Winfrey, Ellen DeGeneres, and Donald Trump.[8] Little wonder that the Celebrity Heat Index, which measures exposure in celebrity news magazines and on websites, is considered major news. *USA Today* publishes its index monthly and makes its annual assessment a major story.[9] And then there is Stefani Joanne Angelina Germanotta, named one of the most influential people in the world by *Time* magazine.

Better known to most as Lady Gaga.

In his book *Fame Junkies*, Jake Halpern asks probing questions in relation to what he calls America's favorite addiction:

> Why do more people watch the ultimate competition for celebrity, *American Idol*, than watch the nightly news on the three major networks combined?
>
> Why do down-to-earth, educated people find stories about Paris Hilton's dating life irresistible?

Why do teenage girls—when given the option of "pressing a magic button and becoming stronger, smarter, famous, or more beautiful"—overwhelmingly opt for fame?[10]

The Celebrification of Culture

One of the more telling cultural shifts of the last seventy-five years has been what some are calling the "celebrification" of culture. It's an awkward term, perhaps, but like industrialization and bureaucratization, it speaks to a broad and historical trend: the increasing centrality of celebrities to the culture. Movie and television stars, professional athletes and musicians, business moguls and journalists have captured our attention as never before.[11]

Daniel J. Boorstin, in his seminal study *The Image*, suggests that the celebrity is a person who is "well-known for his well-known-ness"—or as his quip is often paraphrased, "a celebrity is someone famous for being famous." The celebrity is, writes Boorstin, the "human pseudo-event." This is vastly different from the *hero* who used to fill the role of the modern celebrity. "The hero was distinguished by his achievement; the celebrity by his image or trademark," writes Boorstin. "The hero created himself; the celebrity is created by the media. The hero was a big man; the celebrity is a big name."[12]

Yet now the *celebrity* is the hero. Joseph Epstein writes that "a received opinion about America in the early twenty-first century is that our culture values only two things: money and celebrity."[13] From this, celebrities have become our cultural commentators, charity spokespersons, role models, and political candidates. They have become the arbiters of taste, morality, and public opinion. We live in the "Age of Celebrity," notes Darrell West of Brown University, where "movie stars run for elective office and win. Politicians play fictional characters on television shows. Rock stars raise money for political parties. Musicians, athletes, and artists speak out on issues of hunger, stem cell research, and foreign policy."[14]

The danger, West notes, is that when the press pays closer attention to celebrities speaking out on complex policy subjects than to experts who have detailed knowledge, "politics will be drained of substance, and serious deliberation will be diminished."[15] Yet the media pays attention to celebrities for a simple reason: *we* do. In fact, 2.3 million people buy the *National Enquirer* each week. Another 3.5 million tune in to watch *Inside Edition*. Sites such as TMZ.com are among the most frequented on the Web. As Richard Schickel, who has written for *Time* magazine since 1972, reflects, "No issue or idea in our culture can gain any traction with the general population unless it has celebrity names attached to it."[16]

The new role of celebrity is not without its religious implications. There can be little doubt that many are turning to celebrities to fill a spiritual void. Murray Milner, Jr., professor emeritus of sociology at the University of Virginia, observes the following parallels:

- celebrities, like religious leaders, are usually very charismatic
- religious language and concepts are often invoked by fans who say they worship or idolize celebrities whom they describe as gods or goddesses
- tourists attending a celebrity event in Hollywood are in many ways similar to religious pilgrims at a holy site
- the responses of fans at a rock concert are in many ways comparable to devotees' behaviors at spirit-filled religious events.

When this is coupled with a celebrity actively promoting a particular religion, such as Tom Cruise for Scientology, the influence is staggering.

Christians are not immune to celebrity culture. Some Christians seem to look to Bono as much as Bonhoeffer. Yet influence from a Christian celebrity is only as helpful as the integrity of that celebrity's faith. Singer Jessica Simpson, who was raised by a Baptist minister father and got her start on the Christian music circuit, initially attracted legions of Christian fans. She now says that she rarely goes to church or reads the Bible anymore. "Me and my family got out of that and came to L.A.," she recently commented to a reporter.[17] If you've seen her latest music video, you believe her. Sadly, many young Christian girls have also seen the video and don't know what to believe. Much of the same can be said of Katy Perry, who was also raised by evangelical parents.

Of course the deeper issue may be the way the celebrification of culture is supplanting spirituality. As a Christian devotee of singer Rod Stewart reflected,

> This is something I struggle with. I wish that I were as passionate about Jesus—and the life of Jesus and everything that Jesus said when he was on this earth—as I am about Rod. I do worry about that. I worry that I'm worshiping the celebrity of Rod. And I have to ask myself, Would I really travel across the country to attend a rally for Jesus, like I'm doing for this Walk of Fame event with Rod? I don't know.[18]

The celebrification of culture reflects the deeper needs and longings for that which is transcendent. We are spiritual creatures, and divorced from a relationship with a living God, we will search for *something* spiritual—no matter how passing or trivial—to attempt to satiate our spiritual cravings. Sadly, our culture has reached the point where we are turning to celebrities to fill our spiritual desire.

MISSION

21

Not in Kansas Anymore

I believe in God. I'm not a religious fanatic. I can't remember the last time I went to church. My faith has carried me a long way. It's Sheilaism. Just my own little voice.

Sheila[1]

It's now official. Thanks to the results of the 2010 census, we now know that the United States is, as *USA Today* puts it, "bigger, older, more Hispanic and Asian and less wedded to marriage and traditional families than it was in 1990."

It is also "less enamored of kids, more embracing of several generations living under one roof, more inclusive of same-sex couples, more cognizant of multiracial identities, more suburban, less rural and leaning more to the South and West." As *USA Today* rightly notes,

The end of the first decade of the 21st century marks a turning point in the nation's social, cultural, geographic, racial and ethnic fabric. It's a shift so profound that it reveals an America that seemed unlikely a mere 20 years ago—one that will influence the nation for years to come. . . .

The metamorphosis over just two decades stuns even demographers and social observers.[2]

In 1990, would anyone have predicted that in twenty years we would have a black president? Or a Hispanic population equal to that of a small South American country?

But these pale in comparison to the sweeping change in spiritual sentiment and the significance it holds for the Christian mission.

We're Not in Kansas Anymore

In an article titled "More Americans Tailoring Religion to Fit Their Personal Needs," *USA Today* examined the latest research that indicated that one day 310 million people may have 310 million religions. Today, people are "making up God as they go." "So if World War II–era warbler Kate Smith sang today, her anthem would be '*Gods* Bless America.'"[3]

Adding his lament, *New York Times* columnist David Brooks took note of the findings from the recently released research led by Christian Smith in the book *Lost in Transition*, the third in a series of reports from the largest study of its kind on American youth—specifically, the almost complete inability to think and talk about moral issues. Other than rape and murder, they had a hard time even thinking what else might fall into the *immoral* category, much less what might be moral. Their default position? Moral choices are just a matter of individual taste. "It's personal," the respondents typically said. "It's up to the individual. Who am I to say?" Another typical response: "I would do what I thought made me happy or how I felt. I have no other way of knowing what to do but how I internally feel."[4]

One of the most strategic insights to grasp regarding our day is that we have moved from an Acts 2 cultural context to an Acts 17 cultural context. Both scenes from the New Testament portray a classic engagement of contemporary culture.

In Acts 2:14–39 you have Peter before the God-fearing Jews of Jerusalem. His message is easily paraphrased:

> You know about the creation, Adam and Eve, and the fall; you know about Moses and the law; you know about Abraham and the chosen

people of Israel; you know of the prophets and the promised coming of the Messiah. So we don't need to waste time on that. What you need to know is that Jesus is that Messiah, you rejected him, and now you are in deep weeds and need to repent.

That was it.

And three thousand people repented!

Peter was able to speak to a group of people who were already monotheists, already buying into the Old Testament Scriptures, and already believing in a coming Messiah.

Now move to Acts 17. Paul is on Mars Hill, speaking to the philosophers and spiritual seekers of Athens. Here was a spiritual marketplace where truth was relative, worldviews proliferated, gods littered the landscape, and the average person wouldn't know Abraham from an apricot.

He knew he wasn't in Kansas—I mean Jerusalem—anymore.

So he didn't take an Acts 2 approach, much less give an Acts 2 message. He had to find a way to connect with the culture and the people in it. So he looked around and found a touchstone—an altar to an unknown god. The culture was so pluralistic that the only thing they could agree on was that you couldn't know anything for sure.

"What if I could tell you that unknown god's name? Would that be of interest?"

Paul then went all the way back to creation and worked his way forward—laying a foundation for the understanding and acceptance of the gospel. He had to. They didn't have any knowledge of the Christian faith to start with.

Like today.

But many of us fail to undertake the study Paul made.

Majoring in Secularism

In light of the rising tide of the religious "nones" on the census, one college has decided to be the first to offer a major in secularism. Pitzer College, a small but highly ranked liberal arts institution in Southern California, now offers the major through a new department of secular studies. Professors from a number of departments, including history, philosophy, religion, science, and sociology, teach courses such as "God, Darwin, and Design in America," "Anxiety in the Age of Reason," and "Bible as Literature."

Phil Zuckerman, a sociologist of religion and self-described "agnostic-atheist," proposed the new venture. His interest was sparked by the rising tide of secularism both in the United States and around the world. As mentioned in an earlier chapter, according to the American Religious Identification Survey released in 2009, the percentage of American adults who say they have no religion has doubled in twenty years to 15 percent, constituting the third largest religious group in the nation (eclipsed only by Catholics and Baptists). Zuckerman contends,

> There are hundreds of millions of people who are nonreligious. I want to know who they are, what they believe, why they are nonreligious. You have some countries where huge percentages of people—Czechs, Scandinavians—now call themselves atheists. Canada is experiencing a huge wave of secularization. This is happening very rapidly.

"It has not been studied," he added.[5]

He's right. It hasn't. And it needs to be. And not simply by those who embrace secularism but by those who embrace the Christian faith. We are far more prone to denounce than to discern, to condemn than to comprehend. Those who follow Christ must understand the tenets, causes, and movements of secularism if we are to engage secularism in the marketplace of ideas.

MythBusters

Have you seen the wildly popular show on the Discovery Channel called *MythBusters*? Hosted by Jamie Hyneman and Adam Savage, and cohosted by Tory Belleci, Kari Byron, and Grant Imahara, the MythBusters "mix scientific method with gleeful curiosity and plain old-fashioned ingenuity to create their own signature style of explosive experimentation."[6]

At the time of this writing (through nine years and 189 episodes), they have conducted 2,391 experiments in order to explore 769 myths, such as:

- Does the color red really make a bull angry?
- Can drinking coffee help a person sober up?
- Do most people really use only 10 percent of their brain?
- Is finding a needle in a haystack really that hard?
- Can you be killed by household appliances falling into your bath?
- If an elevator suddenly falls, can you survive by jumping up at the last minute?
- Can someone really knock your socks off?
- Can your cell phone interfere with a plane's instruments?
- Is talking on a cell phone while driving as dangerous as drunk driving?
- Is Chinese water torture effective?
- Can you really freeze your tongue to a pole in cold weather?

Imagine a season during which all they explored were "myths" about the Christian faith in order to determine whether they are true. What should be on the list? At the church I serve, we developed a series titled "Mythbusting," playing off *Mythbusters*, in which we invited attenders to go online and vote on the subjects they most wanted to see examined in light of the Bible and external evidence. We offered a number of ideas from which to choose as well as the opportunity to write in votes. We then took the top six to examine, working our way from the sixth most requested to the number one most requested topic.

The results of the voting:

6. Does God really answer every prayer?
5. Could a boat really hold two of every animal?
4. Can God really forgive anything?
3. Can there really be an antichrist and worldwide tribulation?
2. Does evolution disprove God?
1. Do Christians go to heaven and everyone else to hell?[7]

Then there are the myths already believed that most don't know are a myth. Such as attributing the following statements to the Bible:

- This too shall pass.
- God helps those who help themselves.
- God works in mysterious ways.
- Cleanliness is next to godliness.

The problem? None are in the Bible.
And what about false ideas?

- You wouldn't be having these problems if you were a better Christian.
- Some people can't be forgiven.
- Some prayers go unanswered.
- God's love must be earned.
- Because I'm a Christian, God will protect me from pain and suffering.
- God won't accept me until I have my act together.

Again, not a single biblical idea in the mix.

Mythbusting Series

by James Emery White

Topics include:

- Does God Answer Every Prayer?
- Could a Boat Hold Two of Every Single Animal?
- Can God Really Forgive Anything?
- Can There Really Be an Antichrist and Worldwide Tribulation?
- Does Evolution Disprove God?
- Do Christians Go to Heaven and Everyone Else to Hell?

MP3 and PDF versions available at
http://churchandculture.org/media.asp

Then there are the questions that are often posed as true that suggest an automatic indictment of faith:

- Isn't the Bible full of contradictions and mistakes?
- How can a good and loving God allow so much pain and suffering?
- If Christianity is true, why are there so many hypocrites?

The world of Christian apologetics is in need of a major overhaul. It is too concerned with method, too fixated on winning a debate, and too inclined to bark up the wrong tree (answering questions no one is asking any longer).

Are These Phrases in the Bible?

- "This too shall pass."
- "God helps those who help themselves."
- "God works in mysterious ways."
- "Cleanliness is next to godliness."

Answer: None of these phrases appear in Scripture.

Perhaps we should take a cue from *MythBusters* and employ "plain old-fashioned ingenuity" and provide our own "signature style of explosive experimentation" for a winsome and compelling demonstration of what really is true about the issues people wonder about. Then we may find out what the Discovery Channel did.

People will actually tune in.

But when they do, we'll need to remember where we are standing—and it certainly isn't in Jerusalem.

22

Listening to the Unchurched

Church! Why would I ever go there? They'd just
make me feel even worse than I already do!

Chicago prostitute[1]

Christianity has an image problem.

Many of those outside the Christian faith think Christians no longer represent what Jesus had in mind—that Christianity in our society is not what it was meant to be. Research done by Gabe Lyons and David Kinnaman on how people view the church and people in it found that we are seen as hyperpolitical, out of touch, pushy in our beliefs, and arrogant. And the most common perceptions are that we are homophobic, hypocritical, and judgmental.[2]

Simply put, in the minds of many people, modern-day Christianity no longer seems Christian.

And much of that image has been earned. We've acted in ways, talked in ways, and lived in ways that have tarnished God's reputation.

The heart of the matter is represented in the list that follows. Young Americans outside the church offered these words or phrases as possible descriptors of Christianity, and the percentage shows those who affirmed their accuracy:

- antihomosexual (91 percent)
- judgmental (87 percent)
- hypocritical (85 percent)
- old-fashioned (78 percent)
- too involved in politics (75 percent)
- out of touch with reality (72 percent)
- insensitive to others (70 percent)
- boring (68 percent)
- not accepting of other faiths (64 percent)
- confusing (61 percent)[3]

Fifteen years ago I commissioned a similar study. I asked unchurched people a simple question: How did the church and those inside it lose you? I first published the research, done in coordination with the Barna Research Group, in my book *Rethinking the Church*. (They also conducted the research for *UnChristian*.) Comparing the two studies is interesting.

In 1992 unchurched people gave the following reasons for abandoning the church:

- There is no value in attending (74 percent)
- Churches have too many problems (61 percent)
- I do not have the time (48 percent)
- I am simply not interested (42 percent)
- Churches ask for money too frequently (40 percent)
- Church services are usually boring (36 percent)
- Christian churches hold no relevance for the way I live (34 percent)
- I do not believe in God, or, I am unsure that God exists (12 percent)

Such findings pointed to a culture that was saying, "God, yes; church, no." Current research shows the deepening crisis, for it points to a culture saying, "Christ, perhaps; Christianity and Christians, no."

Listening to the Unchurched

What would the unchurched tell us if we listened? It may surprise you. Let's imagine listening to someone rattle off a few things that, in truth, they very much feel:

1. I do not consider myself (nor do I feel like I am) a "pagan." I mean, *really*? A *pagan*? Not sure I like "unchurched" or "irreligious" either, though it's a step up. Ideally, how about John, or Mark, or Sandra? In other words, use my name.

2. I honestly don't mind it when you invite me to your church or talk to me about God. Just keep it—I don't know—*natural*. Like when we talk about sports or movies. I hate feeling like a project. Let's keep it a conversation between friends and as friends. I could see doing that.

3. Please don't be threatened by my questions. *They really are my questions*, and I've had them for a long time. I hope that if Christianity is true, it can stand up under any amount of intellectual scrutiny. Anyway, I would feel a lot better if you were less threatened when I raise questions. I'm not trying to be a jerk by questioning you; I'm just trying to sort it all out. And that means asking you about all kinds of things. I know sometimes it seems combative or aggressive, but God's questions aren't exactly tame—much less safe. And for me, the answers are *everything*.

4. Don't forget that a lot of my junk is emotional, not just intellectual. And it took a lot for me to say that. I almost don't know how to get into this, but I've been burned, disillusioned, hurt. You may win some of our verbal contests, but it doesn't usually move me forward. It still leaves me feeling cold, mostly because some of the time the intellectual stuff is just a smokescreen for what I'm really battling. Here's the last 5 percent: It's not just whether I can buy into this intellectually but whether I can buy into it relationally. In other words, are you really *safe*?

5. I would like to *belong* before I *believe*. What I mean is that I'd like to experience this a bit before signing on. Is that legal? I hope so. I think that if I could test the waters a bit it would be helpful.

6. There's a lot I don't know, and I know it—like not knowing much about the Bible or Jesus or whatever. Don't make me feel stupid about it. If you could start at the beginning and explain it all to me, that would be great. Like starting with Genesis and moving forward.

7. Can we agree that there's a lot of weird stuff attached to Christianity and the Bible? Okay, it may be true, or real, or whatever, but can we just agree that some of it is a bit—bizarre? For some strange reason it would make me feel better to hear you acknowledge how it all looks and sounds to someone from the outside.

8. What's up with all the scandals? I'm sympathetic to screwing up—I do it all the time. But what makes me want to puke is how they're screwing up while they are telling everybody they don't, or that nobody should, or—you get my point. It makes the whole thing seem like a joke. Just own that you have screwed up (that'd be fine with me, really), or just shut up about *not* doing it. But this parading and posturing and then being exposed—it just turns me off. It makes *me* feel like the spiritual one because at least I don't pretend to be something I'm not!

Reasons People Made the Choice to Abandon the Church

- There is no value in attending (74 percent)
- Churches have too many problems (61 percent)
- I do not have the time (48 percent)
- I am simply not interested (42 percent)
- Churches ask for money too frequently (40 percent)
- Church services are usually boring (36 percent)
- Christian churches hold no relevance for the way I live (34 percent)
- I do not believe in God, or, I am unsure that God exists (12 percent)

---

9. I like it when you help people—care for the poor, house the homeless, tend to the widow, protect the orphan, work for justice against sex-traffickers—that gets my attention and feels authentic. It's also convicting, because I'm not doing much in those areas. I agree with it and write a check now and then, but I'm not on the front lines. When you are, it makes me have to listen to what you have to say, whether I like it or not.

10. I'm really open to it all. More than I let on. In fact, I *want* to feel good about myself spiritually. But I don't think I can ever measure

up. When I really think about God, all I feel is guilt and shame, so I stay away. It would be nice if there was something in all of this that would make me feel like I could—I don't know—come home?

Addressing Self-Delusion

Listening to the unchurched involves far more than information. It means taking that information and assessing fundamental barriers and issues.

And nothing is more important to assess than self-delusion.

Financial blogger Carl Richards of the *New York Times* used to think that helping someone get very clear on their current financial reality was the easy part of financial planning. Once reality was framed, the hard part started—like determining where you want to be in twenty years, and then guessing at such things as the rate of return you will earn and inflation.

He has learned that it's defining reality that's the tough part.

Based on a new study from the Federal Reserve Bank of New York, very few Americans have a clear grasp of their financial reality. For example, only 50 percent of households report having credit card debt, while credit card companies say the number is actually 76 percent of households. The average household also reports credit card debt of $4,700. Lenders, however, report an average balance per household of over $7,100.

Some of this comes from willful ignorance. We don't want to know our credit card balance, so we don't pay attention to it (when you are overweight, the last thing you want to see is a scale). The truth is that you can't make progress if you have no idea where you are starting from. Richards observes, "I've noticed that the biggest difference between people who reach their financial goals and those who don't is knowledge of where they stand in the first place."[4]

This is more than a financial necessity. It's a spiritual one.

Mecklenburg Community Church experiences over 70 percent of its total growth from a unique population: the previously unchurched. It's a staggeringly high number, but it has been consistently this high for many years, tracked carefully through our membership process. One of the secrets to our success is that we understand the self-deception most people are under.

Among the unchurched, spiritual progress can't be made until reality is defined in two very important areas where self-delusion runs high. First, typical unchurched people enter our doors thinking that, in some way or another, they are a Christian. Typically, they aren't. At best they have a cultural Christianity; they have a pseudo-faith that addresses very little of their life. They know *of* God but don't *know* God. Second, the typical unchurched people who begin attending do not consider themselves a sinner. A *mistaker*, yes, but not a sinner.

Understanding these two areas of blindness is critical to speaking into the soul of the unchurched in our culture.

In regard to the first area of blindness, we must navigate a three-stage process: (1) help them realize the vacuous nature of their spiritual life; (2) help them explore authentic spirituality as offered through Christ; and then (3) facilitate that relationship beginning and growing. Or more simply put, they come in thinking they are a Christian, they need to discover they're not, and then we need to help them become one.

As for the second area of deception that blocks spiritual progress, we have the tricky business of helping them see they are more than merely a mistaker; they are a sinner—a person in open moral rebellion against a holy God. And they need to see that the wages of those sins are spiritual death.

This is a stiff drink for the average person of our day.

But unless there is a clear sense of personal sin, coupled with the holiness of God, the very heart of salvation will be waved off with an apathetic wave of the hand. Without a clear sense of sin, grace isn't—well, amazing, much less needed.

So I agree with the financial planners: I've noticed that the biggest difference between churches that have people coming to Christ and those that don't is how adept they are at helping people gain an understanding of where they stand in the first place. Until they know where they are starting from, it is going to be very hard to get them anywhere.

23

No Longer Seeking

> I really have never thought about that. . . . It's been
> fun to get these kinds of questions that I never,
> never think about.
>
> Secularist in Sweden

Can we just drop the word *seeker*?

As in becoming a *seeker church*, being *seeker-targeted* in strategy, talking about reaching *seekers*, or evaluating what a *seeker* may think about our service. Let's not forget about abandoning being *seeker-driven* and *seeker-sensitive*. Don't misunderstand. I've used the term in these and many other ways. But it's a term rooted in the '80s and '90s—irrelevant at best, and terribly misleading at worst.

First, there is the problem with the idea that gave it birth. The term *seeker* referred in a general way to the unchurched who were turned off to church but open to God. Think back to the flood of baby boomers wanting to find a church for their kids but feeling free of the religious and denominational moorings of their youth. These were people who truly were seeking, open to exploring the Christian faith for their life, and often in active search mode.

Newsflash: They've stopped looking.

Most who are outside of the church are not seeking. Confused, maybe; but in active search mode to discover what God may mean for their life? Not too many. Most are just apathetic. The 2008 American Religious Identification Survey offered the following conclusion: "The challenge to Christianity . . . does not come from other religions but from a rejection of all forms of organized religion." Barry Kosmin, coresearcher for the survey, added, "These people aren't secularized. They're not thinking about religion and rejecting it; they're not thinking about it at all."[1]

So much for seeking.

Jonathan Rauch, in an article for the *Atlantic Monthly*, coined a term to describe his own spiritual condition. After a couple of glasses of Merlot, someone asked him about his religion. He was about to say "atheist" when it dawned on him that this wasn't quite accurate. "I used to call myself an atheist," he ended up responding, "and I still don't believe in God, but the larger truth is that it has been years since I really cared one way or another. I'm"—and this was when it hit him—"an . . . apatheist!" Rauch went on to describe his state as a "disinclination to care all that much about one's own religion, and an even stronger disinclination to care about other people's."[2]

He's not alone.

According to the 2011 Baylor University Religion Survey, 44 percent said they spend no time seeking "eternal wisdom." Another 46 percent told Lifeway Research they never wonder whether they will go to heaven. So when it comes to matters related to God, religion, or even atheism, millions simply shrug their shoulders and say, "So what?"[3]

The Fear of Flying

It's been a tough season for the airline industry. Air traffic controllers have been caught sleeping on their night shifts; Southwest airlines found numerous holes that led to the grounding of scores of planes; Air France clipped a smaller jet on the tarmac; a woman was sexually assaulted in a Denver concourse.

If you were already reluctant to fly, this didn't help.

Now compare that to the church. Scandals with pedophile priests; televangelists caught with their hands in the money jar or up someone's skirt; pastors burning Korans; churches splitting over the color of the carpet. If you were already reluctant to attend, this doesn't help either. This brings up the formidable challenge facing those churches that are truly wanting to reach out to those interested in exploring the Christian faith but are turned off to the church.

Let's stay with the airline industry. It is one thing to try to convince people wanting to fly from Charlotte to Atlanta to consider using Delta's services over US Airways. It is another thing altogether to get someone on board who has no desire to fly.

Types of Church Growth

1. Biological Growth—occurs when a child of existing believers with ties to a church comes to faith in Christ through his or her involvement in the church.
2. Transfer Growth—occurs when a Christian moves into an area and chooses to join a church or when a locally churched Christian makes the decision to move to another church home; another term for this is *sheep swapping*.
3. Prodigal Growth—occurs when a person who embraces Christian beliefs has left the life of Christian community but then eventually decides to return to the church.
4. Conversion Growth—occurs when a church reaches a non-Christian, someone who had rejected the truth and claims of Christianity (whether consciously or unconsciously), who then enters into a life-changing, personal relationship with Christ as Savior and Lord.

Switching airlines is akin to *transfer growth*: attracting the already convinced to your church. This is what constitutes most church growth in America. It's sheep swapping. But getting someone averse to flying to step onto the concourse, much less down a boarding ramp, is something altogether different. That's *conversion growth*. This does not represent much of the growth of churches in the United States. Transfer growth is so much easier. These people want to fly! They are just looking for the best airline: best service, best seats, best flight times, best flight attendants, best pilots. They are making a consumer decision. But make no mistake, they are ready to buy.

Conversion growth is much, much tougher. These are people who don't even like airports. And getting them past security, through the concourse, down the ramp, and into seat 15C? Well, let's call it what it is: it's trying to turn atheists into missionaries.

Yet it is possible. There's one thing that 82 percent of all unchurched people can't seem to resist. It cuts through their defenses and penetrates their barriers. According to the research at Lifeway, 82 percent of them seem to have a single weakness: an invitation from a friend or someone they know.

It's worth repeating: 82 percent of all unchurched people would come to church this weekend if invited by a friend.[4]

How strange that we don't invite them.

108

It used to be 130, but now it's 108.

As in the median worship attendance at a typical congregation, which has declined—again—from 130 to 108.

According to a 2011 Hartford Seminary study, "Faith Communities Today," the percentage of congregations with an average weekly worship attendance of 100 or fewer moved from 42 percent to 49 percent. More than a quarter of all congregations had 50 or fewer people in attendance.[5]

Did You Know?

82 percent of all unchurched people would come to church this weekend if invited by a friend.

And the megachurches (congregations with 2,000 or more weekly attendees)?

While the number of megachurches doubled, they only make up 0.5 percent of all congregations. As David Roozen, author of the report "A Decade of Change in American Congregations, 2000–2010" and director of the Hartford Institute of Religion Research, notes, "There are more megachurches but, in fact, they're getting an increasing piece of an overall shrinking pie."[6]

Why is this happening?

It's simple. When we think about growth, we are not thinking about conversion growth. We are thinking about biological growth or transfer growth.

Biological growth occurs when a child of existing believers with ties to a church comes to faith in Christ through his or her involvement in the church. For example, in the southern state of Kerala, India, where Catholics have long been a large minority group, church authorities believe the state's overall Christian population could drop to 17 percent this year, down from 19.5 percent in 1991. Worried about their dwindling numbers, the Roman Catholic Church in southern India announced a campaign to increase attendance by asking its flock to have more babies. It even went so far as to offer free schooling, medical care, and even cash bonuses for large families.[7]

Another way of growing is the aforementioned *transfer growth*.

This takes place when a Christian moves into an area and chooses to join a church, or when a locally churched Christian makes the decision to move to another local church home. Such a person does not come to a church as a nonbeliever, nor does this person come from an unchurched background. At best, he or she is temporarily unchurched due to relocation or some other life issue. This type of growth, then, results from nothing more than the movement of existing believers.

I recall many years ago reading an article about a large church that was experiencing financial difficulty. When asked why the church was stalled in its growth, the pastor replied that when they started, they were the only evangelical church around. Now there were several good Bible-teaching churches.

So people had a choice.

Which was why they weren't growing.

You can also add *prodigal growth* to the mix. A prodigal is someone without a recent church background or church involvement. This person embraces Christian beliefs and, in some cases, has maintained a certain level of spirituality. For one reason or another, however, this person leaves the church and may have lived his or her life outside Christ's daily management and direct, personal leadership. Prodigal growth occurs when a person who has left the life of Christian community returns to the church. Renewal and rededication may take place as part of the return and, at times, even rebaptism.

But missing in most churches' thinking is *conversion growth*. This type of growth occurs when a church reaches a non-Christian. Consciously or not, such a person has rejected the truth and claims of Christianity. To grow through conversion is to grow by reaching a person who has not entered into a life-changing, personal relationship with Christ as Savior and Lord.

If things don't change, small churches will keep getting smaller, big churches will keep attracting larger numbers of the already convinced (often at the expense of the smaller churches), and the Christian population as a whole will remain in decline. That is because the real story of 130 becoming 108 is found in another set of numbers.

Refusing to leave the 99 for the 1.

I cited the telling words of Jonathan Rauch who, in an article for the *Atlantic Monthly*, coined a term to describe his own spiritual condition: *apatheist*, which he described as a "disinclination to care all that much about one's own religion, and an even stronger disinclination to care about other people's."

But then he went on to describe the Christians he knows.

"I have Christian friends who organize their lives around an intense and personal relationship with God, but who betray no sign of caring that I am an unrepentantly atheistic Jewish homosexual. They are exponents, at least, of the second, more important part of apatheism: the part that doesn't mind what other people think about God."[8]

Which is the most hellish apatheism of all.

24

Clash of Civilizations

Where were you when the world stopped turning?

Alan Jackson[1]

In 1995 Thomas Cahill came out with the provocatively titled book *How the Irish Saved Civilization*. "Ireland," contends Cahill, "had one moment of unblemished glory. . . . As the Roman Empire fell, as all through Europe matted, unwashed barbarians descended on the Roman cities, looting artifacts and burning books, the Irish, who were just learning to read and write, took up the great labor of copying all of Western literature."[2]

Then missionary-minded Irish monks brought what had been pre-served on their isolated island back to the continent, refounding European civilization. And that, Cahill concludes, is how the Irish saved civilization. But there is more at hand in Cahill's study than meets the eye. Beyond the loss of Latin literature and the development of the great national European literatures that an illiterate Europe would not have established, Cahill notes that something else would have perished in the West: "the habits of the mind that encourage thought." Why would this matter? Cahill continues his assessment: "And when

Islam began its medieval expansion, it would have encountered scant resistance to its plans—just scattered tribes of animists, ready for a new identity."[3] Without a robust mind to engage the onslaught—and a Christian one at that—the West would have been under the crescent instead of the cross.

The Day After the World Stopped Turning

I think all Americans can tell you exactly where they were and what they were doing that Tuesday morning on September 11, 2001, when they heard the news. Much less is there a single American who can't relive the emotions of seeing it all unfold.

First one plane hit the north tower of the World Trade Center in New York; then, just over twenty minutes later, a second plane hit the south tower; followed by a third plane hitting one of the most secure sites on American soil: the Pentagon in Washington, D.C. All this was followed by the south tower of the World Trade Center collapsing, with reports of people leaping from windows to try to escape. Then the cameras took us back to the Pentagon to see the west side of that building collapse.

Suddenly a fourth plane crashed outside of Pittsburgh. Then the second of the two towers of the World Trade Center collapsed.

And it was no movie; it was the most horrifyingly real national tragedy in American history. Thousands dead. And it unfolded before our very eyes.

But it wasn't just 9/11 that happened. It was 9/12.

As John Allen writes, "The terrorist attacks of September 11, 2001, produced a sea-change in interfaith priorities."

Suddenly, Islam *mattered*.[4]

Press reports about Islam had begun long before the events of September 11 or the name Osama bin Laden and his al-Qaeda network hit the news. From the Ayatollah Khomeini to Louis Farrakhan and the Million Man March, from the death threats on the life of author Salman Rushdie to movies about Malcolm X, from the celebrity conversions of Cassius Clay (now Muhammad Ali) to singer Cat Stevens (now Yusuf Islam), few religions have generated the kinds of discussions and debates, conversations and dialogues, as Islam.

Regardless of world events, it will remain in the news because the Islamic faith is one of the world's two largest religions, second only to Christianity. And it will become much of the heart of the Christian mission. There is great attention on reaching the American unchurched, and rightly so. But such an emphasis must not come at the expense of missing the heart of the global mission, which is to reach the Muslim world.

The Challenge of Muslim Demographics

You may be among the over 13 million to date who have viewed the startling video on YouTube titled "Muslim Demographics." It spread virally with blinding speed.[5]

Here's the short version: the birthrate of non-Muslims compared to Muslims, coupled with immigration, will result in Muslims taking over the planet. According to the video, if Christians want to keep up, we'd better start having babies and amp up our evangelism. And if I got it right, probably in that order. It is a disturbing video. It is designed to alarm, and it does its job well. As you can imagine, the video has already been taken to task for fearmongering and truth-distortion, and to a degree, rightfully so.[6] But it does raise a significant cultural challenge: Islam is on the rise, and its rise is a challenge for Christians throughout the world.

Predicted Growth of Muslims in Europe from 2010 to 2030

- Austria will move from 5.7 percent Muslim to 9.3 percent
- Italy will move from 2.6 percent to 5.4 percent
- Norway will move from 3 percent to 6.5 percent
- Sweden will move from 4.9 percent to 9.9 percent
- the United Kingdom will move from 4.6 percent to 8.2 percent[7]

There are now over 1 billion Muslims in the world. The number of mosques in the United States increased by 42 percent between 1990 and 2000, outpacing both evangelical Protestant denominations and mainline Catholic groups.[8] There are now more Muslims in the United States than there are Episcopalians and as many—if not more—Muslims in the United States than there are Jews. In fact, Muslims are likely to outnumber Christians in Britain in just a few decades.

Clash of Civilizations

Contrary to stereotypes and caricatures, the majority of Muslims are not from the Arab world. The largest numbers are in Indonesia. Further, few Muslims are radical terrorists who want to bomb the world to bits or kill every American in sight. The truth is that during the Persian Gulf War, Islamic nations such as Egypt, Syria, Saudi Arabia, and others joined with Western nations to fight against Islamic Iraq and its invasion of Kuwait. And many—indeed, most—Muslims around the world condemned the terrorist acts on the World Trade Center and the Pentagon.

Yet our world is ablaze with conflict between Islam and the West. Harvard professor Samuel P. Huntington presciently saw this conflict looming on the horizon and called it the "clash of civilizations."[9] Released before 9/11, his book came out at the same time as Francis Fukuyama's *The End of History and the Last Man*, which received most of the press (featuring the idea that all of history had essentially ended with the fall of communism). Huntington's thesis was equally provocative but more widely dismissed—namely that there are three great civilizations (Western, Asian, and Islamic), that there will be great conflict between the West and Islam, and that Islam's militarism will force itself on the world.

This conflict has been fast-tracked due to another demographic. While the Christian population as a whole has remained steady, its distribution has not. Of the 2.18 billion Christians in the world, only 25 percent can be found in Europe. In 1910 about two-thirds of all Christians lived in Europe.

So where have all the Christians gone?

South.

For example, the Christian percentage of the population in sub-Saharan Africa rose from 9 percent in 1910 to 63 percent in 2010. In the Asia-Pacific region it went from 3 percent to 7 percent.[10]

Why does this generate conflict? As an article in the *Economist* noted, "The locus of the world's largest religion is shifting to hotter (in several senses) parts of the world." In Nigeria, scores of Christians have died in Islamist bomb attacks targeting Christmas prayers. In Iran and Pakistan, Christians are being put on death row for *apostasy* (translation: leaving Islam) or *blasphemy*. Dozens of churches in Indonesia have been attacked or shuttered. Two-thirds of Iraq's prewar Christians have fled. In Egypt and Syria, Muslim zeal threatens ancient Christian groups.[11]

And it's not just happening in other parts of the world.

Consider a tale of two ads. It is a simple, almost benign story, but one that bookends the past year and reflects the growing sentiment of our land.

In 2011 football phenomenon and committed Christian Tim Tebow began his strained relationship with the secular media by agreeing to do a pro-family ad sponsored by Focus on the Family for the Super Bowl. It was met with howls of protest by many who said that there was no place for such ads on television. Boycotts were called for against the network in the hope that they would cancel the ad.

Later that same year, Lowe's decided to pull its ads from a reality show on TLC about Muslim-Americans due to complaints from Christian groups that the show was promoting Islam as a faith. Once again there was a reaction, but against the home improvement chain. Calling the retail giant's decision "un-American" and "naked . . . bigotry," Democratic California State Senator Ted Lieu told the Associated Press he was even considering legislative action if Lowe's didn't apologize to Muslims and reinstate the ads.[12]

All this to say that Fukuyama was proven wrong.

Huntington was proven right.

The Real Challenge of Demographics

But as Timothy George posed, "Is the God of Muhammad the Father of Jesus?" The answer, George writes, is surely yes and no. Yes, in the sense that the Father of Jesus is the only God there is. He is the Creator and Sovereign Lord of Muhammad, Buddha, Confucius, and every person who has ever lived. But the answer is also no because Muslim theology rejects the divinity of Christ and the personhood of the Holy Spirit—both essential components of the Christian understanding of God.[13]

So the challenge of Muslim demographics is the challenge of outreach to Muslims. But can they be reached?

From 1991 to 2007, Fuller Theological Seminary's School of Intercultural Studies conducted a survey among 750 Muslims who had converted to Christianity. Those surveyed represented fifty ethnic groups from thirty different countries. The most cited reason for conversion to the Christian faith was the message of grace. They said that Christians appeared to have loving marriages in which women were treated as equals; that the Koran had produced profound disillusionment because it accentuates "God's punishment more than his love, and the use of violence to impose Islamic laws." Even further, they said as Muslims they could never be as certain of their forgiveness and salvation as Christians can.

Did You Know?

From 1991 to 2007 Fuller Theological Seminary's School of Intercultural Studies conducted a survey among 750 Muslims who had converted to Christianity. The most cited reason for the conversion to the Christian faith?

Grace.

Philip Yancey writes about a British conference on comparative religions. Experts from around the world debated what, if any, belief was unique to the Christian faith. They began by eliminating possibilities.

Is it the incarnation?

No—other religions have different versions of gods appearing in human form.

Is it the resurrection of Jesus?

Again, other religions have accounts of return from death.

The debate went on for some time until the famed Christian author C. S. Lewis wandered into the room, asking what the debate was about. He was told that his colleagues were discussing Christianity's unique contribution among world religions.

Lewis responded, "Oh, that's easy. It's grace."

After some discussion, the conferees had to agree.[14]

And that is precisely the unique dynamic that Muslims most need to hear.

25

Whatever Happened to Evangelism?

> Jesus said, "Adolph! Why did you do the ugly, evil
> things you did? Why were you so cruel?"
> "Because nobody ever told me how much you
> loved me."
>
> Martin Niemoller, recurring dream[1]

In 1973 psychiatrist Karl Menninger published a book with the provocative title *Whatever Became of Sin?* His point was that sociology and psychology tend to avoid terms like *evil*, *immorality*, and *wrongdoing*. Menninger details how the theological notion of sin became the legal idea of crime and then slid further from its true meaning when it was relegated to the psychological category of sickness.

It's time someone wrote a book for the church titled *Whatever Became of Evangelism?* The point would be how we tend to avoid terms like *lost*, *hell*, or *salvation*. It would detail how the Great Commission became the Great Rhetoric and then finally fell into the category of the Great Community. It wouldn't take long to lay out how it all happened. It fits nicely into a short equation:

Virtue of Tolerance + Emphasis on Social Ministry = Diminished Evangelism

Let's break the equation down.

First, *tolerance.*

There is little doubt that tolerance is our culture's uber-virtue. Specifically, tolerance defined as "acceptance of other people's beliefs" and lifestyle; then, defining acceptance as "equally valid."

This flows from a confusion about the idea of tolerance. When we speak of tolerance, we usually mean social tolerance: "I accept you as a person." Or at times, legal tolerance: "You have the right to believe what you wish." We do not, however, tend to mean *intellectual* tolerance. This would mean that all ideas are equally valid. Virtually no one believes that ideas supporting genocide, pedophilia, racism, sexism, or the rejection of the historical reality of the Holocaust should be tolerated. But it is precisely the idea of intellectual tolerance we find ourselves sloppily embracing under the overarching mantra of tolerance.

The dilemma with such a position, as T. S. Eliot rightly points out, is that "it is not enthusiasm, but dogma, that differentiates a Christian from a pagan society."[2]

Then there is our emphasis on *social ministry.*

In what is arguably a reaction against the previous generation's emphasis on social morality—namely abortion and same-sex marriage—younger Christians (and now older ones as well) are giving renewed emphasis to matters of social justice, including a new interest in public policies that address issues related to peace, health, and poverty. The reaction is not hard to understand. Few eras of American Christian history are reviled as much as the Moral Majority of the 1980s and its attempt to impose Christian values on culture through political maneuvering. The idea at the time was simple and attractive: if we could only have Christians in the White House, Congress, and the Supreme Court, or populating other leadership elites, then morality would be enacted and faith would once again find the fertile soil needed to establish its footing in individual lives.

Formula for the Breakdown of Evangelism

Virtue of Tolerance + Emphasis on Social Ministry = Diminished Evangelism

Three Types of Tolerance

- Social tolerance—accepting another person for who he or she is regardless of what that person believes
- Legal tolerance—everyone has the basic first amendment right to believe what he or she wants to believe
- Intellectual tolerance—accepting what someone believes as *right* regardless of what you believe or think is right; all ideas are equally valid

The moral majority "won" through the election of Ronald Reagan as president, and his subsequent Supreme Court appointments throughout the 1980s brought great anticipation for substantive change. Yet there has been little real change to mark as a result. Even the prime target—the striking down of the Supreme Court decision *Roe v. Wade*, which legalized abortion—remains the law of the land to this day. What *was* achieved was cultural division and Christians feeling more vilified than ever. The "culture wars" of the 1980s and 90s are now widely viewed as some of the more distasteful episodes in recent memory, and many younger evangelicals want nothing to do with what was often a caustic, abrasive, and unloving approach toward those apart from Christ.

So what is the result of tolerance as the supreme virtue coupled with a new emphasis on social justice?

We'll buy Tom's Shoes, but not witness to Tom.

Let's get the necessary qualifier out of the way. Social ministry should not be pitted against evangelism. We should extend the Bread of Life as well as bread for the stomach. But we must never begin and end with the stomach alone.

I suspect some of this is tied to our need to be accepted by the secular culture. The scandal of the cross—and humanity's desperate need for it—doesn't play as well as the hip work of the International Justice Mission or supporting Bono in Africa. We get a taste of doing something that plays well in culture, and we become like Sally Field at the Oscars: "You like me! You really, really like me!"

We should lock eyes with the poor and the hungry, the sex-traffic victim and the destitute. We should care for them deeply and serve

---

What Are Tom's Shoes?

In 2006, American traveler Blake Mycoskie befriended children in Argentina and found they had no shoes to protect their feet. Wanting to help, he created TOMS Shoes, a company that matches each pair of shoes purchased with a pair of new shoes given to a child in need. One for One.

Source: toms.com/our-movement

---

them in the name of Christ. But we must not forget to give them Christ. Because once this life is over, the food we gave them for their stomach will mean nothing compared to the food we gave them for their souls. How tragic it would be to have compassion for the immediate needs of this life but not the eternal needs of the life to come.

So yes, buy a pair of Tom's Shoes.

Just don't forget Tom.

The Gift of a Bible

"But what if I turn them off?" "What if they react negatively?" This seems to be the arresting fear of our day, but it is an unfounded anxiety. Most people—even the most hardened of skeptics—respond positively to a winsome and compelling witness.

Penn Jillette is the talkative half of Penn and Teller, the Las Vegas comedy-illusion team, now with their own program on Showtime titled *Penn and Teller: Bulls***!* Penn is an outspoken atheist. But he posted a video blog on his personal website about a man who gave him a Bible, and it has much to teach Christians:

> I want to talk to you about this. I got home from a show and at the end of the show, as I've mentioned before, we go out and we talk to folks, you know, sign an occasional autograph and shake hands and so on. And there was one guy waiting over to the side in what I call the "hover position" after I was all done. Big guy, probably about my

age. Big guy. And he had been the guy who picks the joke during our psychic comedian section of the show. So he had the props from that in his hand because we give those away. He had the joke book, the envelope, and the paper, and stuff. . . .

And he walked over to me and he said, "I was here last night at the show, and I saw the show and I liked the show. . . ." He was very complimentary about my use of language and complimentary about honesty and stuff. He said nice stuff, no need to go into it, he said nice stuff.

And then he said, "I brought this for you," and he handed me a Gideon pocket edition. I thought it said from the New Testament but also, Psalms is from the New Testament, right? Little book . . . about this big, this thick. And he said, "I wrote in the front of it and I wanted you to have this, I'm kind of proselytizing." And then he said, "I'm a businessman. I'm sane; I'm not crazy." And he looked me right in the eye and did all of this. And it was really wonderful.

I believe he knew that I was an atheist. But he was not defensive. And he looked me right in the eyes. And he was truly complimentary . . . it didn't seem like empty flattery. He was really kind and nice and sane and looked me in the eyes and talked to me and then gave me this Bible. And I've always said that I don't respect people who don't proselytize. I don't respect that at all. If you believe that there is a heaven and hell and that people could be going to hell or not getting eternal life or whatever, and you think that, well, it's not really worth telling them this because it would make it socially awkward . . . and atheists who think that people shouldn't proselytize, just leave me alone, keep your religion to yourself . . . uh . . . How much do you have to hate somebody to not proselytize? How much do you have to hate somebody to believe that everlasting life is possible and not tell them that?

I mean, if I believed beyond a shadow of a doubt that a truck was coming at you and you didn't believe it, but that truck was bearing down on you, there's a certain point where I tackle you. And this is more important than that. And I've always thought that and I've written about that and I've thought of it conceptually.

This guy was a really good guy. He was polite, and honest, and sane, and he cared enough about me to proselytize and give me a Bible. Which he had written in it a little note to me . . . just like, liked your show and so on. And then like five phone numbers for him and an email address if I wanted to get in touch. Now, I know there's no God. And one polite person living his life right doesn't change that. But I'll tell ya, he was a very, very, very good man. And that's real important. And with that kind of goodness it's okay to have that deep of a disagreement. I still think that religion does a lot of bad stuff. But man, that was a really good man who gave me that book. That's all I wanted to say.[3]

And perhaps that's all we need to hear.

Afterword

Acting on a Lesser God

The writer Douglas Coupland, who coined the term *Gen X*, offers a bleak picture of the future. Calling himself a "radical pessimist," he's created a "Radical Pessimist's Guide to the Next 10 Years."[1]

Of the "tips for survival in a messed-up future," the first one is to recognize that "it's going to get worse"; the last is that "we will accept the obvious truth that we brought this upon ourselves." In between are a bunch of glass-half-empty insights and predictions that include technological determinism, extreme weather, the fragmentation of North America, stupid people being in charge of everything, the end of fresh vegetables, and IKEA being an ever more spiritual sanctuary for us all.

Most of us are well aware that the future will be VUCA (volatile, uncertain, complex, and ambiguous). But as Kevin Roberts notes, it's easy to make that same assessment from the point of view of the optimist.

> At numerous points throughout history, it was easy to make gloomy predictions about the future. . . . Whether it was World War II, the bursting of the dot-com bubble, or the aftermath of 9/11. And yet time and again, we find ways of banding together, harnessing our creativity, and not just persevering but thriving. The challenges of the future

will no doubt be novel, but they won't be insurmountable. Whether it's breakneck technological change, environmental sustainability, or economic turnarounds, these are issues that need to be met with radical optimism and the conviction that nothing is impossible.[2]

Roberts obviously flirts with a utopian vision that is out of synch with a fallen world and the depravity of human beings. This was, of course, the mistake of Enlightenment thinkers who felt that human progress was unlimited and could solve the world's problems. But two world wars, marked by Auschwitz and Hiroshima, proved that we needed far more than technological advancement to address the ills of this world.

But does this mean we join with Coupland's sentiments? Many Christians would. Not his predictions, per se, and they certainly wouldn't call themselves pessimists. But they would embrace the idea that the world is in an inevitable downward spiral, and there is little worth doing beyond being faithful and persevering to the end.

But isn't there a place for hope, and a life that lives accordingly, regardless of your view of the end times?

The crisis is upon us, and so is the need for those with the spiritual drive and determination to meet the challenge. Historian Richard Landes once noted that there are two ways to look at the unfolding of history as we approach its inevitable end: as roosters or as owls.

> Roosters crow about the imminent dawn. Apocalyptic prophets, messianic pretenders, chronologists calculating an imminent doomsday—they all want to rouse the courtyard, stir the animals into action. . . . Owls are night animals; they dislike both noise and light; they want to hush the roosters, insisting that it is still night, that the dawn is far away, that the roosters are not only incorrect, but dangerous.[3]

As authors Robert Clouse, Robert Hosack, and Richard Pierard wrote in the heat of millennium fever approaching the year 2000, reflecting on Landes's contention, we "embrace the rooster's call to action," but we argue that "no one knows about that day or hour" (Mark 13:32).[4] Even further, Paul wrote to Timothy that Christ is our hope (1 Tim. 1:1), a hope that speaks to our salvation and the assurance that God's kingdom and purposes will prevail (see Acts 2:26; Rom. 8:24–25; Titus 1:2).

But there is more for us here than a theology of hope rooted in eschatology. There is hope in the life to come, to be sure, but also for the life at hand. And specifically, hope that we can effect change, make a difference with our life, and expand the kingdom of God on earth during our lifetime. Not in a utopian delusion, but in a robust understanding that there is a God on the loose.

The great epitaph in Acts for David was that he served God's purposes for his generation (Acts 13:36). While not wanting anyone to presume on the future, James encourages us to do all the good we can while we still have breath (James 4:13–17), a sentiment echoed by the psalmist (Psalm 90) and the apostle Paul (Ephesians 5).

And what will happen when we give of our lives this way?

Jesus speaks of what can happen with a poppy seed of faith mixed with action (Matt. 17:14–21, Message). He tells us that with God all things are possible (Matt. 19:16–28) and that with faith, mountains can be moved (Matt. 21:18–21). The Great Commission is nothing less than Jesus putting audacious vision into the act of mission (Matt. 28:16–20). As C. S. Lewis once observed, the New Testament contains what can only be called embarrassing promises of what our lives can unleash through prayer, faithfulness, and action.

The problem is that most of us don't pray to that God. We don't embrace his vision. We don't believe in those promises. It is as if we have decided on a lesser god, and as a result, we are more likely to accept the list of predictions from a radical pessimist than we are to embrace the promises of Jesus.

So we come full circle.

The men of Issachar didn't simply understand the times. They took that understanding and began to formulate what to do.

And there is so much we can do.

Notes

Introduction

1. In addition to the Galileo quote, see Daniel J. Boorstin, *The Discoverers: A History of Man's Search to Know His World and Himself* (New York: Random House, 1983), 314.

2. Ibid., 327–29.

3. Jean-Francois Paul de Gondi, Cardinal de Retz, *Memoires*, bk. 2 (1717; repr., Middlesex: Echo, 2007), cited by Fred R. Shapiro, ed., *Yale Book of Quotations* (New Haven: Yale University Press, 2006), 633–34.

4. Christopher Dawson, "The Six Ages of the Church," in *Christianity and European Culture*, ed. Gerald J. Russello (Washington: Catholic University of America Press, 1998), 34–45.

5. For this, I am indebted to Vincent Strudwick, "God in Oxford," in *Theology and Spirituality: An Introduction to Themes at the University of Oxford Summer Programme in Theology, 2003*, ed. John Morgan and Jane Shaw (Richmond, Indiana: GTF Books, 2003), 1–4.

6. "'Bad Day' Is Top One-Hit Wonder," Associated Press, as reported in the *Charlotte Observer*, December 8, 2009, 2A. For link to *Billboard* announcement, see http://www.billboard.com/charts/hot-100#/news/daniel-powter-is-decade-s-top-one-hit-wonder-1004051688.story.

7. "The Decade from Hell," *Time*, December 7, 2009, cover.

8. Jonathan Weisman, "Voter Discontent Deepens Ahead of Obama Jobs Plan," *Wall Street Journal*, September 6, 2011; online at http://online.wsj.com/article/SB100014240 53111903895904576547014053423394.html?mod=WSJ_Election_MIDDLETopStories.

Chapter 1 A Post-Christian America

1. Flannery O'Connor, "Some Aspects of the Grotesque in Southern Fiction," in *Mystery and Manners: Occasional Prose*, selected and edited by Sally and Robert Fitzgerald (New York: Farrar, Straus, and Giroux, 1969), 44.

2. James Poniewozik, "Generation X-Mas: How an Upstart Film Became a Holiday Icon for the Post-Boomer Set," *Time*, December 10, 2007, 90; available online at http://www.time.com/time/magazine/article/0,9171,1689235,00.html.

3. Ibid.

4. National Religious Broadcasters analysis can be found in the Winter 2004 edition of *Enrichment* and also on the website of *Preaching Today* (a service of *Christianity Today* magazine). The website for the NRB is www.nrb.org.

5. David Klinghoffer, "That Other Church," *Christianity Today*, January 2005, 62.

6. See James Emery White, *Serious Times: Making Your Life Matter in an Urgent Day* (Downers Grove, IL: InterVarsity Press, 2004).

7. Paul M. Zulehner quoted by Uwe Siemon-Netto, "Analysis: Atheism Worldwide in Decline," United Press International, March 1, 2005, http://www.upi.com/Business_News/Security-Industry/2005/03/01/Analysis-Atheism-worldwide-in-decline/UPI-20691109700930/.

8. Cathy Lynn Grossman, "Almost All Denominations Losing Ground: Faith Is Shifting, Drifting or Vanishing Outright," *USA Today*, March 9, 2009, 1A, 6A; Rachel Zoll, "Survey: We're Losing Our Religion," Associated Press, March 9, 2009, printed in the *Charlotte Observer*, March 9, 2009, 5A; "America Becoming Less Christian, Survey Finds," CNN, March 12, 2009, http://www.cnn.com/2009/LIVING/wayoflife/03/09/us.religion.less.christian/index.html; Lance Dickie, "U.S. Religion ID Inching to 'None'," *Seattle Times*, printed in the *Charlotte Observer*, March 24, 2009, 11A; Adelle M. Banks, "None of Thee Above," Religious News Service, printed in the *Charlotte Observer*, 1E, 3E, March 14, 2009.

9. For a précis on the ARIS study, along with links to the full survey, go to http://www.americanreligionsurvey-aris.org.

10. Cathy Lynn Grossman, "'Nones' Now 15% of Population, *USA Today*, March 9, 2009, www.usatoday.com/news/religion/2009-03-09-aris-survey-nones_N.htm.

11. Phil Zuckerman, *Society without God* (New York University Press, 2008). See also Peter Steinfels, "A Land of Nonbelievers, Which Is Not to Say Atheists," *New York Times*, February 28, 2009, A15.

12. Stephen Prothero, "A Nation of Religious Illiterates," *Christian Science Monitor*, January 20, 2005, www.csmonitor.com/2005/0120/p09s02-coop.html.

13. Joseph Cardinal Ratzinger, *Salt of the Earth: The Church at the End of the Millennium* (San Francisco: Ignatius, 1997).

14. "Ratzinger, in Final Pre-Conclave Homily, Warns Cardinals of 'Dictatorship of Moral Relativism,'" April 18, 2005, http://www.lifesitenews.com/news/ratzinger-in-final-pre-conclave-homily-warns-cardinals-of-a-dictatorship-of.

15. David McCullough, *John Adams* (New York: Simon and Schuster, 2001), 647.

16. On the history of the idea of America as a chosen nation, see Conrad Cherry, *God's New Israel: Religious Interpretations of American Destiny* (Chapel Hill, NC: University of North Carolina Press, 1998), 29.

17. Peter Marshall and David Manuel, *The Light and the Glory* (New York: Fleming H. Revell, 1977).

18. Mark A. Noll, Nathan O. Hatch, and George M. Marsden, *The Search for Christian America* (Colorado Springs: Helmer and Howard Publishers, 1989).

19. See the writings of Os Guinness.

Chapter 2 Why Johnny Can't Pray

1. Harry Blamires, *The Christian Mind: How Should a Christian Think?* (Vancouver, BC: Regent College Publishing, 2005), 3.

2. "Most Americans Believe in God but Don't Know Religious Tenets," *USA Today*, September 29, 2010; online at http://www.usatoday.com/news/religion/2010-09-28-pew28_ST_N.htm?loc=interstitialskip.

3. Stephen Prothero, *Religious Literacy: What Every American Needs to Know* (San Francisco: HarperSanFrancisco, 2007).

4. John Blake, "Actually, That's Not in the Bible," CNN, June 5, 2011; online at http://religion.blogs.cnn.com/2011/06/05/thats-not-in-the-bible/?hpt=hp_cl.

5. Alex Pappas, "Richard Wolffe Makes Fun of Palin for Reading Famous Author of Christian Works for 'Divine Inspiration,'" *Daily Caller*, December 9, 2010; online at http://dailycaller.com/2010/12/09/richard-wolffe-makes-fun-of-palin-for-reading-famous-author-of-christian-works-for-%E2%80%98divine-inspiration%E2%80%99.

6. Roger Lancelyn Green and Walter Hooper, *C. S. Lewis: A Biography*, rev. ed. (New York: Harcourt, 1974), 209.

7. C. S. Lewis, *Mere Christianity* (New York: HarperCollins, 2001), ix.

8. Rosa Prince, "Bishop of Winchester: Legal System Discriminates against Christians," *The Telegraph*, December 26, 2010, http://www.telegraph.co.uk/news/newstopics/religion/8225991/Bishop-of-Winchester-legal-system-discriminates-against-Christians.html.

9. Laura Roberts, "The Christians Who Felt Discriminated Against," *The Telegraph*, December 27, 2010; online at http://www.telegraph.co.uk/news/newstopics/religion/8226444/The-Christians-who-felt-discriminated-against.html.

10. Stephen Prothero, "We Live in the Land of Biblical Idiots," March 14, 2007, http://www.latimes.com/news/opinion/commentary/la-oe-prothero14mar14,1,3102398.story. See also Cathy Lynn Grossman, "Americans Get an 'F' in Religion," *USA Today*, http://www.usatoday.com/news/religion/2007-03-07-teaching-religion-cover_N.htm.

11. E. D. Hirsch, *Cultural Literacy: What Every American Needs to Know* (New York: Random House, 1988).

12. James Emery White, *A Mind for God* (Downers Grove, IL: InterVarsity Press, 2006).

13. Alister McGrath, *The Twilight of Atheism* (New York: Doubleday, 2004), xi.

14. John R. W. Stott, *Your Mind Matters: The Place of the Mind in the Christian Life* (Downers Grove, IL: InterVarsity Press, 1972), 13.

Chapter 3 The Church of the Jedi

1. Francis A. Schaeffer, *Escape from Reason* (Downers Grove, IL: InterVarsity Press, 2006), 25.

2. Paul Froese and Christopher Bader, *America's Four Gods: What We Say about God—and What That Says about Us* (Oxford: Oxford University Press, 2010).

3. Benjamin Franklin, "Articles of Belief and Acts of Religion, First Principles," 1728, quoted in http://www.historycarper.com/resources/twobf2/articles/htm.

4. Froese and Bader, *America's Four Gods*, 143.

5. Rodney Stark, *Discovering God: The Origins of the Great Religions and the Evolution of Belief* (New York: HarperCollins, 2007), 10.

6. For further discussion about Oprah, see Robert J. Thompson, Jennifer Harris, and Elwood Watson, *The Oprah Phenomenon* (Lexington, KY: University Press of Kentucky, 2007); Robin Westen, *Oprah Winfrey: I Don't Believe in Failure*, African American Biography Series (Berkeley Heights, NJ: Enslow Publishers, 2005); Marcia Nelson, *The Gospel According to Oprah* (Louisville, KY: Westminster John Knox Press, 2005); LaTonya Taylor, "The Church of O," posted April 1, 2002, *Christianity Today*, www.christianitytoday.com/ct/2002/april1/1.38.html.

7. On the thought of Eckhart Tolle, see his books *The Power of Now: A Guide to Spiritual Enlightenment* (Vancouver, BCL Namaste Publishing, 1999); *Stillness Speaks* (Namaste, 2003); and *A New Earth: Awakening Your Life's Purpose* (New York: Penguin, 2005).

8. Tolle, *A New Earth*, 71.

9. Ibid., 292.

10. "'Star Wars' Chosen as Religion in Czech Republic on New Census," *Huffington Post*, December 18, 2011, http://www.huffingtonpost.com/2011/12/18/star-wars-a-religion-in-czech-republic_n_1156516.html.

Chapter 4 Unfortunate Godmongering

1. Jean-Paul Sartre, *Existentialism and Human Emotions* (New York: Kensington Publishing, 1957), 63.

2. Ian Sample, "Stephen Hawking: 'There Is No Heaven; It's a Fairy Story,'" *The Guardian*, May 15, 2011; online at http://www.guardian.co.uk/science/2011/may/15/stephen -hawking-interview-there-is-no-heaven.

3. Stephen W. Hawking, *A Brief History of Time* (New York: Bantam Books, 1988).

4. Dwight Garner, "Many Kinds of Universes, and None Require God," *New York Times*, September 8, 2010, C1; online at http://www.nytimes.com/2010/09/08/books/08book. html?scp=8&sq=Dwight%20Garner&st=cse.

5. Harry Blamires, *The Christian Mind*, 44.

6. Stephen W. Hawking and Leonard Mlodinow, *The Grand Design* (New York: Random House Group, 2010), 8.

7. Jane Hawking, *Traveling to Infinity: My Life with Stephen* (United Kingdom: Alma Books, 2008).

8. Cornelia Dean, "Evolution Book Sees No Science-Religion Gap," *New York Times*, January 4, 2008, A11.

9. "*Science, Evolution and Creationism*," Committee on Revising Science and Creationism: A View from the National Academy of Sciences, National Academy of Sciences and Institute of Medicine of the National Academies. Available as a free PDF from http://www. nap.edu/catalog/11876.html.

10. Elaine Howard Ecklund, "Science on Faith," *Chronicle Review*, February 11, 2011, B9–10.

11. Ian Barbour, *When Science Meets Religion: Enemies, Strangers, or Partners?* (London: SPCK, 2000), xi.

12. For an informed critique of many of the more popular aspects of applied naturalism, see Phillip E. Johnson, *Reason in the Balance: The Case against Naturalism in Science, Law and Education* (Downers Grove, IL: InterVarsity Press, 1995).

13. For further discussion, see Chris Mooney and Sheril Kirshenbaum, *Unscientific America: How Scientific Illiteracy Threatens Our Future* (New York: Basic Books, 2009), 103–4.

14. Carl Sagan, *The Demon-Haunted World: Science as a Candle in the Dark* (New York: Random House, 1995).

15. David C. Lindberg and Ronald L. Numbers, *When Science and Christianity Meet* (Chicago: University of Chicago Press, 2003), 278.

16. See Seth Borenstein, "Planet in Sweet Spot of Goldilocks Zone for Life," Associated Press, *Charlotte Observer*, December 5, 2011; online at http://www.charlotteobserver. com/2011/12/05/2828577/nasa-finds-planet-thats-just-about.html; Dan Vergano, "Earthlike Planet Discovered in 'Habitable' Zone," *USA Today*, December 5, 2011; online at http://www.usatoday.com/tech/science/space/story/2011-12-05/nasa-finds-planet-that-could-sustain-life/51656310/1; Andy Bloxham, "Kepler 22b—the 'New Earth'—Could Have Oceans and Continents, Scientists Claim," *Daily Telegraph*, December 6, 2011; online at http://www.telegraph.co.uk/science/space/8939138/Kepler-22b-the-new-Earth-could-have-oceans-and-continents-scientists-claim.html.

17. See also Lee Strobel's film series "The Case for a Creator," specifically 33:27–36:31.

18. There is some dispute as to whether Gagarin said this or if it was Khrushchev's comment in a later speech.

19. Alan Guth, *The Inflationary Universe: The Quest for a New Theory of Cosmic Origins* (New York: Perseus Books, 1997), 276.

20. John Polkinghorne and Nicholas Beale, *Questions of Truth* (Louisville: Westminster John Knox, 2009), 5–9.

21. Michael Wenham, "I'd Stake My Life that Stephen Hawking Is Wrong about Heaven," *The Guardian*, May 17, 2011; online at http://www.guardian.co.uk/commentisfree/belief/2011/may/17/stephen-hawking-heaven.

22. Alicia Cohn, "Lady Gaga: Where's the Outrage?" May 17, 2011, *Christianity Today*; online at http://blog.christianitytoday.com/women/2011/05/the_real_outrage_of_lady_gaga.html.

23. Wenham, "I'd Stake My Life that Stephen Hawking Is Wrong about Heaven."

Chapter 5 Pseudo-Orthodoxy

1. G. K. Chesteron, *The Autobiography of G. K. Chesterton* (San Francisco: Ignatius Press, 2006), 217.

2. Michael Hinton, *The 100-Minute Bible* (Canterbury, England: The 100-Minute Press, 2005), 5.

3. Alan Hamilton and Ruth Gledhill, "The Slimline Bible that Leaves Out All Those Boring Bits," *Times Online*, September 22, 2005, http://www.thetimes.co.uk/tto/news/uk/article1938488.ece; Jonathan Petre, "The Bible for Slow Readers" *News Telegraph*, September 22, 2005, http://www.telegraph.co.uk/news/uknews/1498893/The-Bible-for-slow-readers.html; Ed Vulliamy, "For the Busy Faithful, the Greatest Story Ever Told—in 100 Minutes," *The Guardian*, September 22, 2005, http://www.guardian.co.uk/uk/2005/sep/22/religion.books; Jesse Noyes, "Publishers See the Light, Put Out Quick-Read Bibles," *Boston Herald*, October 6, 2005; Bernard O'Riordan, "It's gr8 news 4 believers—da Bible sent 2 u in txt," *The Guardian*, October 7, 2005, http://www.guardian.co.uk/world/2005/oct/07/australia.religion; "Bible cre8td for a nu wrl: testaments by SMS," *Sydney Morning Herald*, October 6, 2005, http://www.smh.com.au/news/national/bible-cre8td-for-a-nu-wrl-testaments-by-sms/2005/10/06/1128562927820.html.

4. National Study of Youth and Religion, http://www.youthandreligion.org/research.

5. Christian Smith, *Soul Searching: The Religious and Spiritual Lives of American Teenagers* (repr., New York: Oxford University Press, 2009), 171.

6. Smith, *Soul Searching*, 171.

7. Ibid.

8. Allan Bloom, *The Closing of the American Mind: How Higher Education Has Failed Democracy and Impoverished the Souls of Today's Students* (New York: Simon and Schuster, 1987), 25.

9. Mark A. Noll, *The Scandal of the Evangelical Mind* (Grand Rapids: Eerdmans, 1994).

10. M. L. Denton, L. D. Pearce, and C. Smith, *Religion and Spirituality on the Path through Adolescence, Research Report Number 8*, National Study of Youth and Religion (Chapel Hill, NC: University of North Carolina at Chapel Hill, 2008), www.youthandreligion.org/sites/youthandreligion.org/files/imported/publications/docs/w2_pub_report_final.pdf.

11. Jean Bethke Elshtain in the afterword to *Evangelicals in the Public Square*, ed. J. Budziszewski (Grand Rapids: Baker Academic, 2006), 204.

12. Miguel De La Torre, "A Pop Quiz for Biblical Literalists," Associated Baptist Press, May 7, 2009, http://www.abpnews.com/content/view/4066/9.

13. Ibid., used by permission of Associated Baptist Press.

Chapter 6 The Divine Supermarket

1. Michel Eyquem de Montaigne, *Essays*, book 2, chap. 12 (1580), cited by Shapiro, *Yale Book of Quotations*, 533.

2. Rabbi Marc Gellman and Monsignor Thomas Hartman, *How Do You Spell God?* (New York: Morrow Junior Books, 1995), 19–24.

3. Peter Berger, *The Sacred Canopy: Elements of a Sociological Theory of Religion* (New York: Anchor Books, 1967), 127. The historical background to this stream of modernity is charted in Nathan O. Hatch, *The Democratization of American Christianity* (New Haven: Yale, 1989).

4. Berger, *Sacred Canopy*, 94. The idea of religion as a canopy serves as the motif for Martin E. Marty's exploration of modern American religion, *Modern American Religion: The Irony of It All, 1893–1919* (Chicago: University of Chicago Press, 1986), the first of several volumes on twentieth-century American religion.

5. For one of the most thorough and insightful treatments of issues related to this in regard to Christian thought and enterprise, see Harold Netland, *Encountering Religious Pluralism: The Challenge to Christian Faith and Mission* (Downers Grove, IL: InterVarsity Press, 2001).

6. Langdon Gilkey, *Through the Tempest: Theological Voyages in a Pluralistic Culture* (Minneapolis: Fortress Press, 1991), 21.

7. Harold O. J. Brown, "Evangelicals and Social Ethics," *Evangelical Affirmations,* ed. Kenneth S. Kantzer and Carl F. H. Henry (Grand Rapids: Academie/Zondervan, 1990), 279.

8. Malise Ruthven, *The Divine Supermarket: Travels in Search of the Soul of America* (London: Tauris Parke Paperbacks, 2012).

9. John Blake, "Four Ways 9/11 Changed America's Attitude toward Religion," CNN, September 3, 2011; online at http://religion.blogs.cnn.com/2011/09/03/four-ways-911-changed-americas-attitude-toward-religion.

10. Ibid.

11. Douglas V. Steere, *On Being Present Where You Are*, Pendle Hill Pamphlet no. 151 (Wallingford, PA: Pendle Hill, 1967), 22.

12. Harold A. Netland, *Dissonant Voices: Religious Pluralism and the Question of Truth* (Grand Rapids: Eerdmans, 1991), 30.

13. Bloom, *Closing of the American Mind*, 26.

14. Timothy Shortell, "Religion and Morality: A Contradiction Explained," *Fifteen Credibility Street*, www.anti-naturals.org/theory/religion.html.

15. Jacob Gershman, "Professor Who Belittled Believers Drops Bid to Head Up a Department," *New York Sun*, June 8, 2005, http://www.nysun.com/new-york/professor-who-belittled-believers-drops-bid/15053/; "Top Prof Sparks Outrage," *New York Daily News*, May 23, 2005, http://articles.nydailynews.com/2005-05-23/local/18301076_1_brooklyn-college-student-religious-people; Shoshana Baum, "Anti-Religion Prof's Promotion Rankles Brooklyn Campus," *Jewish Week*, June 3, 2005, http://www.highbeam.com/doc/1P1-112534139.html.

16. As chronicled by Mooney and Kirshenbaum, *Unscientific America*, 95–97.

17. Christopher Hitchens, *God Is Not Great: How Religion Poisons Everything* (New York: Hachette Book Group, 2007), 56.

18. Ibid., 283.

Chapter 7 Neomedieval

1. George Eliot, *Scenes of Clerical Life* (1858), cited by Shapiro, *Yale Book of Quotations*, 614.

2. What follows is an abbreviated discussion of a more fulsome treatment in my earlier book, *Serious Times* (Downers Grove, IL: InterVarsity Press, 2004).

3. Thomas Cahill, *How the Irish Saved Civilization* (New York: Nan Talese/Doubleday, 1995).

4. Douglas Coupland, *Life after God* (New York: Pocket Books, Simon and Schuster, 1995), 359.

5. Umberto Eco, *Travels in Hyper Reality: Essays*, trans. William Weaver (San Diego: Harcourt Brace Jovanovich, 1986), 73.

6. John Skinner, trans., *The Confession of Saint Patrick* (New York: Image/Doubleday, 1998). There are only two surviving works that can be attributed to Patrick: his *Confessio* (Confession) and his *Epistola* (Letter to Coroticus); see also Maire B. De Paor, *Patrick: The Pilgrim Apostle of Ireland* (New York: Regan/HarperCollins, 1998).

7. Cahill, *How the Irish Saved Civilization*, 131.

8. See Martina Bagnoli, Holger A. Klein, C. Griffith Mann, and James Robinson, eds. *Treasures of Heaven: Saints, Relics, and Devotion in Medieval Europe* (London: British Museum Press, 2010).

9. John Calvin, *Traite des reliques*, ed. A. Autin (Paris, 1921).

Chapter 8 The New American Dream

1. Erich Fromm, *Escape from Freedom* (New York: Henry Holt, 1994), 115.

2. Neil Howe, William Strauss, and R. J. Matson, *Millennials Rising: The Next Great Generation* (New York: Vintage, 2000).

3. Francisco Vara-Orta, "Majority of Freshmen View Gay Marriage as OK," *Los Angeles Times*, posted on latimes.com, January 19, 2007, http://pqasb.pqarchiver.com/latimes/access/1196768071.html?dids=1196768071:1196768071&FMT=ABS&FMTS=ABS:FT&type=current&date=Jan+19%2C+2007&author=Francisco+Vara-Orta&pub=Los+Angeles+Times&edition=&startpage=B.4&desc=Majority+of+freshmen+view+gay+marriage+as+OK.

4. Sharon Jayson, "The Goal: Wealth and Fame," *USA Today*, January 10, 2007, 1–2D; online at http://www.usatoday.com/news/nation/2007-01-09-gen-y-cover_x.htm.

5. "How the New Generation of Well-Wired Multitaskers Is Changing Campus Culture," Information Technology section, *Chronicle of Higher Education*, January 5, 2007, B10–15.

6. Jayson, "The Goal: Wealth and Fame."

7. Ibid.

8. Neal Gabler, "The New American Dream," *Boston Globe*, March 31, 2011; online at http://www.boston.com/bostonglobe/editorial_opinion/oped/articles/2011/03/31/the_new_american_dream.

9. Ibid.

10. Ibid.

11. Ibid.

12. Christian Smith, et al., *Lost in Transition: The Dark Side of Emerging Adulthood* (Oxford: Oxford University Press, 2011), 92.

13. Ibid., 74, 76, 94–96.

14. Christopher Lasch, *The Culture of Narcissism: American Life in An Age of Diminishing Expectations* (New York: W. W. Norton, 1991), 7.

15. Philip Rieff cited in Roger Lundin, *From Nature to Experience: The American Search for Cultural Authority* (New York: Rowman and Littlefield, 2007), 24.

16. Stanley J. Grenz, *A Primer on Postmodernism* (Grand Rapids: Eerdmans, 1996), 62.

17. Michael Burleigh, *The Third Reich: A New History* (New York: Hill and Wang/Farrar, Straus and Giroux, 2000), 1.

18. H. R. Rookmaaker, *Modern Art and the Death of a Culture* (Wheaton: Crossway, 1994), 61.

19. See White, *Serious Times*.

20. Jean M. Twenge, *Generation Me: Why Today's Young Americans Are More Confident, Assertive, Entitled—and More Miserable Than Ever Before* (New York: Free Press, 2006), 1.

Chapter 9 Wikiworld

1. Saul Bellow, from the foreword to Bloom, *Closing of the American Mind*, 17.

2. Brock Read, "'Wikimania' Participants Give the Online Encyclopedia Mixed Reviews," *Chronicle of Higher Education*, September 1, 2006, A62.

3. For a direct link to Colbert's take on Wikiality, see http://www.comedycentral.com/motherload/index.jhtml?ml_video=72347.

4. Jacques Steinberg, "2005: In a Word; Truthiness," *New York Times*, December 25, 2005, http://query.nytimes.com/gst/fullpage.html?res=9F0CE6D81530F936A15751C1A9639C8B63.

5. Ibid., 21.

6. Thomas Friedman, *The World Is Flat: A Brief History of the Twenty-First Century* (New York: Farrar, Straus and Giroux, 2005), 10.

7. Don Tapscott and Anthony Williams, *Wikinomics: How Mass Collaboration Changes Everything* (New York: Penguin Books, 2007), 1.

8. Ibid., 3.

9. See the *Time* article at http://www.time.com/time/magazine/article/0,9171,1569514,00.html?aid=434&from=o&to=http%3A//www.time.com/time/magazine/article/0%2C9171%2C1569514%2C00.html.

10. Thomas Oden, *After Modernity . . . What?* (Grand Rapids: Zondervan, 1990), 74.

11. Jacques Barzun, *From Dawn to Decadence: 500 Years of Western Cultural Life, 1500 to the Present* (New York: HarperCollins, 2000), xv.

12. Andrew Keen, *The Cult of the Amateur: How Today's Internet Is Killing Our Culture* (New York: Doubleday, 2007), 16–17.

13. Neil Postman, *Technopoly: The Surrender of Culture to Technology* (New York: Alfred A. Knopf, 1992).

14. Jacques Ellul, *The Technological Society*, trans. John Wilkinson (New York: Vintage Books, 1964).

15. On the meaning of the words *techne* and *technites*, see J. I. Packer, "Carpenter, Builder, Workman, Craftsman, Trade," in *The New International Dictionary of New Testament Theology*, vol. 1, ed. Colin Brown, Regency Reference Library (1975, repr., Grand Rapids: Zondervan, 1986), 279.

16. Anjana Ahuja, "God Is Not in Charge, We Are," *Times*, London, July 24, 2003, 6.

Chapter 10 Forgetting How to Blush

1. D. H. Lawrence, *Studies in Classic American Literature*, ch. 8 (1923), cited by Shapiro, *Yale Book of Quotations*, 445.

2. "Top Pop Songs 2nd April, 2011," http://charter.hubpages.com/hub/Top-Pop-Songs-2011.

3. Karl Menninger, *Whatever Became of Sin?* (New York: Hawthorn Books, 1973).

4. For a video and full transcript of the Gammons interview, go to http://sports.espn.go.com/mlb/news/story?id=3895281.

5. National Center for Health Statistics, Sexual Behavior and Selected Health Measures: Men and Women 15–44 Years of Age, United States, 2002. For the full report, go to http://www.cdc.gov/nchs/products/pubs/pubd/ad/361-370/ad362.htm.

6. Claire Brindis quoted in Laura Sessions Stepp, "Study: Half of All Teens Have Had Oral Sex," *Washington Post*, September 16, 2005, www.washingtonpost.com.

7. "Is Teen Parenthood Glamorized on MTV?" *Today Show*, NBC, September 16, 2010, http://today.msnbc.msn.com/id/26184891/vp/39209845#39209845.

8. Smith, *Lost in Transition*, 21.

9. Ibid., 22, 30, 38, 47, 48, 51.

10. James Tozer, "Is It a Sin? Christian Words Deleted from Oxford Dictionary," *Daily Mail*, December 7, 2008; online at http://www.dailymail.co.uk/news/article-1092668/Is-sin-Christian-words-deleted-Oxford-dictionary.html#.

11. Mark MacKinnon, "China's 'Moral Qualities' Need Improving, Leaders Say," *Globe and Mail*, October 19, 2011, A11.

12. Tim Gardam, "Christians in China: Is the Country in Spiritual Crisis?" BBC News, September 11, 2011; online at http://www.bbc.co.uk/news/magazine-14838749.

Chapter 11 Just Not into Marriage

1. Quoted by Twenge, *Generation Me*, 3.

2. Conor Dougherty, "New Vow: I Don't Take Thee," *Wall Street Journal*, September 29, 2010, A3.

3. Jennifer Ludden, "When It Comes to Marriage, Many More Say 'I Don't,'" National Public Radio, December 14, 2011, http://www.npr.org/2011/12/14/143660764/when-it-comes-to-marriage-many-more-say-i-dont.

4. Dougherty, "I Don't Take Thee," A3.

5. Sabrina Tavernise, "More Unwed Parents Live Together, Report Finds" *New York Times*, August 16, 2011; online at http://www.nytimes.com/2011/08/17/us/17cohabitation.html?_r=1&src=rechp.

6. Robert Preidt, "Living Together Too Much Commitment for Today's Couples," *USA Today*, August 7, 2011; online at http://yourlife.usatoday.com/sex-relationships/dating/story/2011/08/Living-together-too-much-commitment-for-todays-couples/49849606/1.

7. "Mexico City Considers Two-Year Marriages," *Fox News Latino*, October 3, 2011; online at http://latino.foxnews.com/latino/news/2011/10/03/mexico-city-considers-two-year-marriages/?test=latestnews#ixzz1bdJ18mdr.

8. "Are We in a Culture of Divorce?" *Today Show*, January 15, 2011; online at http://today.msnbc.msn.com/id/26184891/vp/41089989#41089989.

9. AOL mainpage, Wednesday morning, March 19, 2003.

10. Jim Daly, "Marriage in Obsolescence," *Christianity Today*, November 20, 2010; online at http://www.christianitytoday.com/ct/2010/novemberweb-only/55-52.0.html.

11. Ross Douthat, "The Changing Culture War," *New York Times*, December 6, 2010; online at http://www.nytimes.com/2010/12/06/opinion/06douthat.html?_r=1&ref=rossdouthat.

12. Glenn T. Stanton and Dr. Bill Maier, *Marriage on Trial* (Downers Grove, IL: InterVarsity Press, 2004), 12.

13. James Q. Wilson, *The Marriage Problem: How Our Culture Has Weakened Families* (New York: Harper Collins, 2002), 16.

14. Stanton and Maier, *Marriage on Trial*, 100.

15. Christine Armario, "1 in 4 American Children Raised by a Single Parent," Associated Press, April 27, 2011, http://www.msnbc.msn.com/id/42780551/ns/health-childrens_health/t/american-children-raised-single-parent/#.T7RTSlKuMTA.

16. Mary Parke, "Are Married Parents Really Better for Children?" Center for Law and Social Policy Policy Brief, May 2003, 1.

17. James C. Dobson, *Home with a Heart* (Carol Stream, IL: Living Books, 1999), 86–87.

18. For further insight into Coolidge's views, see the article in *Crisis* magazine, cited by Charles Colson, "Why Not Gay Marriage?" *Christianity Today*, October 28, 1996.

19. Timothy George, "What Is the Gospel Response to the Prop. 8 Decision?" *Christianity Today*, August 2010; online at http://www.christianitytoday.com/ct/2010/augustweb-only/42.11.0.html.

20. See Tom Curry, "High Court Could Make Gay Marriage a 2012 issue," MSNBC, June 29, 2011, http://www.msnbc.msn.com/id/43581652/ns/politics; Adam Liptak, "A Tipping Point for Gay Marriage?" *New York Times*; April 30, 2011, http://www.nytimes.com/2011/05/01/weekinreview/01gay.html?src=rechp.

21. "Cameron Diaz Doesn't Want to Be with One Guy Forever" PopEater Staff, July 22, 2010, http://www.popeater.com/2010/07/22/cameron-diaz-dating-love/?icid =main|htmlws-main-n|dl2|link4|http%3A%2F% 2Fwww.popeater.com%2F2010%2F07% 2F22%2Fcameron-diaz-dating-love%2F.

Chapter 12 Pornification

1. David Hume, "On Impudence and Modesty" in *Essays: Moral, Political and Literary,* cited by Wendy Shalit, *A Return to Modesty: Discovering the Lost Virtue* (New York: Touchstone, 1999), 15.

2. Stephanie Rosenbloom, "The Taming of the Slur," *New York Times*, July 17, 2006, E1, E7.

3. Ibid.

4. Ibid.

5. Ibid.

6. Leora Tanenbaum, *Slut! Growing Up Female with a Bad Reputation* (New York: HarperCollins, 2000).

7. On the sexualization of Halloween, see Stephanie Rosenbloom, "Good Girls Go Bad, For a Day," *New York Times*, October 19, 2006, E1–2; Maria Puente, "Halloween Décor Is Getting Christmassy," *USA Today*, October 13, 2006, D1.

8. Tara Kelly, "PETA Plans a Porn Site," *Huffington Post*, August 19, 2011, http://www.huffingtonpost.com/2011/08/19/peta-porn-site_n_931509.html.

9. "Kids See Sex on TV, Not the Web," *Baptist Press*, August 8, 2011; online at http://www.bpnews.net/BPnews.asp?ID=35902.

10. Frank Rich, cited by Candice M. Kelsey, *Generation MySpace: Helping Your Teen Survive Online Adolescence* (New York: Marlowe and Company, 2007), 205.

11. Juliann Garey quoted in Shalit, *Return to Modesty*, 49–50.

12. Pamela Paul, *Pornified: How Pornography Is Transforming Our Lives, Our Relationships, and Our Families* (New York: Times Books, 2005).

13. Ibid.

14. On statistics related to pornography, see http://internet-filter-review.toptenreviews.com/internet-pornography-statistics.html.

15. Nerve.com, "The Prurient Interest: An Eighth Grader Weighs In," October 10, 2006, cited by Keen, *Cult of the Amateur*, 158–59.

16. C. S. Lewis, *Mere Christianity* (New York: HarperCollins, 2001), 96.

Chapter 13 Modern Family

1. Sigmund Freud, *Letter to an American Mother*, April 9, 1935, cited by Shapiro, *Yale Book of Quotations*, 291.

2. Evelyn Lilly, "Cultural Rhythms Showcases Talent," *Harvard Crimson*, News Section, February 28, 2005; online at http://www.thecrimson.com/article/2005/2/28/cultural-rhythms-showcases-talent-actress-jada.

3. Anna M. Friedman, "Pinkett Smith's Remarks Debated," *Harvard Crimson*, News Section, March 2, 2005; online at http://www.thecrimson.com/article/2005/3/2/pinkett-smiths-remarks-debated-after-some.

4. Jocelyn Noveck, "New Facebook Status Options Applauded by Gay Users" *USA Today*, February 19, 2001; online at http://www.usatoday.com/tech/news/2011-02-19-facebook-partner-status_N.htm.

5. Liptak, "Tipping Point for Gay Marriage?" Andrew Malcolm, "A First: Majority of Americans Now Supports Same-Sex Marriage, Gallup Finds," *Los Angeles Times*, May 20, 2011; online at http://latimesblogs.latimes.com/washington/2011/05/gay-marriage-ok-with-majority-of-americans-gallup.html; Patrick McGreevy, "Assembly Passes Bill to Require Contributions of Gays in Textbooks," *Los Angeles Times*, July 6, 2011; online at http://www.latimes.com/news/local/la-me-gay-rights-20110706,0,3768798.story.

6. Christi Parsons and Tom Hamburger, "Has Backing Gay Marriage Lost Its Political Risk?" *Charlotte Observer*, February 27, 2011, 19A–20A; online at http://www.charlotteobserver.com/2011/02/27/2095463/has-backing-gay-marriage-lost.html.

7. Cathleen Falsani, "Is Evangelical Christianity Having a Great Gay Awakening?" *The Huffington Post*, January 12, 2011; online at http://www.huffingtonpost.com/cathleen-falsani/the-great-gay-awakening_b_808235.html.

8. George Lucas, cited in Michael Medved, *Hollywood vs. America* (New York: HarperCollins, 1993), 271.

9. American Association of Christian Counselors Law and Ethics Committee, *AACC Code of Ethics: The Y2004 Final Code*, 2004, Section 1-126, page 9.

10. Sheryl Gay Stolberg, "Christian Counseling by Hopeful's Spouse Prompts Questions," *New York Times*, July 16, 2011; online at http://www.nytimes.com/2011/07/17/us/politics/17clinic.html?src=rechp.

11. Ibid.

12. Quoted in Liptak, "Tipping Point for Gay Marriage?"

13. Patti Zarling, "High School Newspaper Column Sparks Controversy," *Green Bay Press-Gazette*, featured in *USA Today*, January 15, 2012; online at http://www.usatoday.com/news/nation/story/2012-01-15/gay-parenting-shawano/52567228/1.

Chapter 14 Regarding Gender

1. Francis Fukuyama, *Our Posthuman Future* (New York: Picador, 2002), 217–18.

2. Linton Weeks, "The End of Gender," National Public Radio, June 23, 2011; online at http://www.npr.org/2011/06/24/137342682/the-end-of-gender.

3. Beverly White and Bill French, "UCLA Considers 'Gender Inclusive' Dorms," NBC-Los Angeles, October 13, 2011; online at http://www.nbclosangeles.com/news/local/UCLA-Considers-Controversial-Dorm-Plan-131496963.html.

4. Steven Rhoads, *Taking Sex Differences Seriously* (San Francisco: Encounter Books, 2004).

5. Perry Chiaramonte, "Transgender Girl Scout Controversy Sheds Light on Organization's 'Inclusive' Policies," Fox News, October 28, 2011, http://www.foxnews.com/us/2011/10/28/transgender-youth-brings-to-light-policies-within-girl-scouts/.

6. Ibid.

7. Ibid.

8. C. S. Lewis, *The Abolition of Man* (1947, repr., New York: Collier/Macmillan, 1955), 77.

Chapter 15 The Disappearance of Childhood

1. Neil Postman, *The Disappearance of Childhood* (New York: Vintage Books, 1994), ix.

2. Steve Bird, "'Miss Bimbo' Web Site Sparks Outrage in Britain," *London Times*/Fox News, March 26, 2008, http://www.foxnews.com/story/0,2933,341284,00.html.

3. Ibid.

4. Joe Piazza, "French Designer Blurs Line between Adulthood and Childhood with New 'Loungerie' Line for Children," Fox News, August 17, 2011; online at http://www.foxnews.com/entertainment/2011/08/17/french-designer-blurs-line-between-adulthood-and-childhood-with-new-loungerie/?test=faces; "Lingerie Line for Little Girls Sparks Outrage," *Today Show*, August 18, 2011: online at http://today.msnbc.msn.com/id/26184891/vp/44187436#44187436.

5. Pamela Paul, "The Playground Gets Even Tougher," *New York Times*, October 8, 2010; online at http://www.nytimes.com/2010/10/10/fashion/10Cultural.html?pagewanted=1&ref=homepage&src=me.

6. Ibid.

7. Ibid.

8. Postman, *Disappearance of Childhood*.

Chapter 16 Supersaturation

1. George Orwell, *1984* (New York: Plume, 2003), part. 1, chap. 5.

2. "The Most Influential Figures in American History," *Atlantic Monthly*, December 2007; online at http://www.theatlantic.com/doc/200612/influentials.

3. Allan Lazar, Dan Karlan, and Jeremy Salter, *The 101 Most Influential People Who Never Lived* (New York: William Morrow, 2006).

4. Ibid., 276.

5. Ibid.

6. Ibid., 277.

7. "'Friends' Cast Had 85 Sexual Partners Over 10-Season Run," Fox News, July 28, 2011, http://www.foxnews.com/entertainment/2011/07/28/friends-cast-had-85-sexual-partners-over-10-season-run/.

8. Fred Fedler, *An Introduction to the Mass Media* (Australia: Harcourt Publishers Group, 1978), 7.

9. Kathleen Parker, "Polls Point to Lack of Parenting," *Sarasota Herald-Tribune*, July 2, 1997; available online at http://news.google.com/newspapers?nid=1755&dat=19970702&id=oTIcAAAAIBAJ&sjid=YH0EAAAAIBAJ&pg=5185,1022827.

10. On ways the media are often less than open, see Bernard Goldberg, *Bias: A CBS Insider Exposes How the Media Distort the News* (Washington: Regnery, 2002); Mark C. Carnes, *Past Imperfect: History According to the Movies* (New York: Henry Hold and Company, 1995).

11. "Oliver Stone: Forget Facts; Films Aren't about Accuracy," Newsmakers, *Charlotte Observer*, September 23, 1997, 2A.

12. Quoted by R. Serge Denisoff, *Inside MTV* (New Brunswick: Transaction Books, 1988), 241.

13. Tamar Lewin, "Children Awake? Then They're Probably Online," *New York Times*, January 20, 2010, A1, A3; online at http://www.nytimes.com/2010/01/20/education/20wired.html?scp=1&sq=Children%20Awake?%20%20Then%20They're%20Probably%20Online&st=cse; Greg Toppo, "Kids' Digital Day: Almost 8 Hours," *USA Today*, January 20, 2010, 1A.

14. Todd Gitlin, *Media Unlimited: How the Torrent of Images and Sounds Overwhelms Our Lives* (New York: Metropolitan Books, 2001), 6, 94.

15. Ibid.

16. Marshall McLuhan with Quentin Fiore, *The Medium Is the Message: An Inventory of Effects* (1967, repr., Corte Madera, CA: Gingko Press, 2001), 26.

17. Gitlin, *Media Unlimited*, 3–5, 128.

18. Matt Richtel, "Growing Up Digital, Wired for Distraction," *New York Times*, November 21, 2010, A1, A20; online at http://www.nytimes.com/2010/11/21/technology/21brain.html?scp=10&sq=Matt%20Richtel&st=cse.

Chapter 17 Homo Interneticus

1. John Freeman, *The Tyranny of E-Mail: The Four-Thousand Year Journey to Your Inbox* (New York: Scribner, 2009), 4.

2. Nathan Olivarez-Giles, "Facebook Had 1 Trillion Page Views in June, According to Google," *Los Angeles Times*, August 25, 2011; online at http://latimesblogs.latimes.com/technology/2011/08/facebook-1-trillion-hits-google.html.

3. "Pew: Half of US Adults Now Use Social Networks," Associated Press, Yahoo! News, August 26, 2011, http://news.yahoo.com/pew-half-us-adults-now-use-social-networks-191020282.html.

4. Figures from Internet World Stats, http://www.internetworldstats.com/top20.htm.

5. Don Tapscott, *Growing Up Digital: The Rise of the Net Generation* (New York: McGraw-hill, 1998).

6. Brian X. Chen, *Always On: How the iPhone Unlocked the Anything-Anytime-Anywhere Future—and Locked Us In* (Cambridge, MA: DaCapo Press, 2011).

7. Graeme Paton, "Children Becoming 'Addicted' to Computers," *Telegraph*, January 2, 2012; online at http://www.telegraph.co.uk/education/educationnews/8988082/Children-becoming-addicted-to-computers.html.

8. Lee Siegel, *Against the Machine: How the Web Is Reshaping Culture and Commerce—and Why It Matters* (New York: Spiegel and Gray, 2008), 7.

9. "Multitasking May Not Mean Higher Productivity," *Talk of the Nation*, NPR, August 28, 2009, www.npr.org/templates/story/story.php?storyId=112334449.

10. Nicholas Carr, *The Shallows: What the Internet Is Doing to Our Brain* (New York: Norton, 2011), 120.

11. Tim Challies, *The Next Story: Life and Faith after the Digital Revolution* (Grand Rapids: Zondervan, 2011), 117.

12. Ibid., 127.

13. Daniel Boorstin, *Cleopatra's Nose: Essays on the Unexpected*, ed. Ruth Boorstin (New York: Random House, 1994), 7.

14. Siegel, *Against the Machine*, 7.

15. From the Pew Research Center's Internet and American Life Project, reported by the *Los Angeles Times*, "What Are You Doing on the Web? Most Under 30 Are Wasting Time," December 2, 2011; online at http://latimesblogs.latimes.com/technology/2011/12/pew-report-53-of-people-under-30-go-.

16. Maggie Jackson, *Distracted: The Erosion of Attention and the Coming Dark Age* (New York: Prometheus, 2009), 13.

17. Emma Barnett, "Social Network Overuse 'Breeds Narcissism,'" *Telegraph*, August 9, 2011.

18. Lewin, "Children Awake?" *New York Times*.

19. "People More Likely to Lie When Texting, Study Finds," *Los Angeles Times*, December 20, 2011; online at http://latimesblogs.latimes.com/technology/2011/12/people-more-likely-to-lie-when-texting-study.html.

20. David Aikman, "Attack Dogs of Christendom," *Christianity Today*, August 27, 2007, www.christianitytoday.com/ct/2007/august/23.52.html.

21. Lee Siegel, *Against the Machine*, 172.

Chapter 18 New News

1. Dominic Rushe, "How Twitter Has Become the People's Voice on the Eve of Its Fifth Birthday," *theguardian/TheObserver*, February 13, 2011; online at http://www.guardian.co.uk/technology/2011/feb/13/twitter-peoples-voice-fifth-birthday.

2. Shane Richmond, "Twitter Announces 100 Million Global Users," *Telegraph*, September 9, 2011; online at http://www.telegraph.co.uk/technology/twitter/8750812/Twitter-announces-100-million-global-users.html.

3. Kate Bussman, *A Twitter Year: 365 Days in 140 Characters* (New York: Bloomsbury, 2011), introduction; see also "'A Twitter Year' In Review: 365 Days, 140 Characters," NPR Books, December 31, 2011; online at http://www.npr.org/2011/12/31/144445325 /a-twitter-year-in-review-365-days-140-characters.

4. Rushe, "How Twitter Has Become the People's Voice."

5. Verne G. Kopytoff, "Blogs Wane as the Young Drift to Sites Like Twitter," *New York Times*, February 20, 2011; online at http://www.nytimes.com/2011/02/21/technology/internet/21blog.html?_r=2&hp.

6. See Laura Oliver, "How Twitter Made the News in 2011," *Guardian*, December 28, 2011; online at http://www.guardian.co.uk/world/blog/2011/dec/28/2011-twitter-news-year.

7. John Dyer, "Not Many of You Should Presume to Be Bloggers," *Christianity Today*, March 11, 2011; online at http://www.christianitytoday.com/ct/2011/marchweb-only/bloggers.html.

8. David Carr, "A Vanishing Journalistic Divide," *New York Times*, October 10, 2010; online at http://www.nytimes.com/2010/10/11/business/media/11carr.html?_r=2&hp.

9. *CNN Headline News*, September 6, 1997.

10. "Some Perspective, Please," *WORLD*, September 20, 1997, 9.

11. Ibid.

12. Cass Sunstein, *Republic.Com* (Princeton: Princeton University Press, 2001).

Chapter 19 Is Google God?

1. Thomas L. Friedman, "Is Google God?" *New York Times*, June 20, 2003.

2. Tim Berners-Lee, *Weaving the Web: The Original Design and Ultimate Destiny of the World Wide Web* (New York: HarperCollins, 1999), 1.

3. See googlezeitgeist.com.

4. Quentin J. Schultze, *Habits of the High-Tech Heart* (Grand Rapids: Baker, 2002).

5. Gary D. Myers, "Theological Ed. Is 'Being Redefined,'" *Baptist Press*; online at http://www.bpnews.net/bpnews.asp?id=35098.

6. "Origins, Meanings and Practices of Easter," http://www.religioustolerance.org/easter.htm.

7. Anthony McRoy, "Was Easter Borrowed from a Pagan Holiday?" April 2009, http://www.christianitytoday.com/ch/bytopic/holidays/easterborrowedholiday.html.

8. As of November 2008, the last reckoning on the site itself.

9. James Altucher, "10 Things I Didn't Know about Steve Jobs," *Business Insider*, August 23, 2011; online at http://www.businessinsider.com/10-unusual-things-i-didnt-know-about-steve-jobs-2011-2#ixzz1WAcDVU32.

Chapter 20 Celebrification

1. Cited by Gitlin, *Media Unlimited*, 141.

2. DeWayne Wickham, "Actor's Daughter, Like So Many Others, Seeks Stardom at a High Cost," *USA Today*, August 10, 2010, 9A.

3. Ibid.

4. CNN/Time Poll conducted June 14–15, 2000, reported at www.pollingreport.com/hollywoo.htm.

5. Quoted by Jake Halpern, *Fame Junkies: The Hidden Truths Behind America's Favorite Addiction* (New York: Houghton Mifflin, 2007), xx.

6. Tom Maurstad, "Living in a People Magazine Culture," *Dallas Morning News*, repr., *Charlotte Observer*, August 31, 2005.

7. See http://www.googlezeitgeist.com/top-lists/us/overall/#/en.

8. For the 2011 Gallup results, see http://www.gallup.com/poll/151790/Barack-Obama-Hillary-Clinton-Again-Top-Admired-List.aspx.

9. Lorena Blas and Mary Cadden, "Kim Kardashian Nets Top Spot in 2011 Heat Index," *USA Today*, January 2, 2012; online at http://www.usatoday.com/life/people/celebwatch/story/2012-01-02/2011-celebrity-heat-index-kim-kardashian/52344622/1.

10. Halpern, *Fame Junkies*, xvi.

11. "Celebrity Culture," *The Hedgehog Review: Critical Reflections on Contemporary Culture* 7, no. 1 (Spring 2005). Articles referenced include: Joseph Epstein, "Celebrity Culture"; Wendy Kaminer, "Get a Life: Illusions of Self-Invention"; Darrell M. West, "American Politics in the Age of Celebrity"; Murray Milner, Jr., "Celebrity Culture as a Status System"; and Jennifer L. Geddes, "An Interview with Richard Schickel."

12. Daniel J. Boorstin, *The Image: A Guide to Pseudo-Events in America* (New York: Vintage, 1992), 221, xlvii, xlii.

13. Joseph Epstein, *In a Cardboard Belt!: Essays Personal, Literary, and Savage* (New York: Houghton Mifflin, 2007), 364.

14. Darrell M. West, "Celebrity Culture in America," August 23, 2011, available online at www.insidepolitics.org/DWestPubs.html.

15. Ibid.

16. Jennifer L. Geddes, "An Interview with Richard Schickel," The Hedgehog Review 7, no. 1 (2005): 82.

17. Entertainment News Staff, "Jessica Simpson Rarely Goes to Church," Softpedia, September 6, 2005, news.softpedia.com/news/Jessica-Simpson-Rarely-Goes-To-Church-7783.shtml.

18. Quoted by Halpern, *Fame Junkies*, 164.

Chapter 21 Not in Kansas Anymore

1. Quoted by Robert Bellah, *Habits of the Heart: Individualism and Commitment in American Life* (Los Angeles: University of California Press, 2007), 221.

2. Haya El Nasser and Paul Overberg, "Census Tracks 20 Years of Sweeping Change," *USA Today*, August 10, 2011; online at http://www.usatoday.com/news/nation/census/2011-08-10-census-20-years-change_n.htm.

3. Cathy Lynn Grossman, "More Americans Tailoring Religion to Fit Their Needs," *USA Today*, September 13, 2011, 2A; online at http://www.usatoday.com/news/religion/story/2011-09-14/america-religious-denominations/50376288/1; see also George Barna, *Futurecast* (Carol Stream, IL: Tyndale, 2011).

4. David Brooks, "If It Feels Right . . . ," *New York Times*, September 12, 2011; online at http://www.nytimes.com/2011/09/13/opinion/if-it-feels-right.html?src=rechp; see also Smith, *Lost in Transition*.

5. Laurie Goodstein, "Pitzer College in California Adds Major in Secularism," *New York Times*, May 7, 2011; online at http://www.nytimes.com/2011/05/08/us/08secular.html?_r=2&src=rechp.

6. "Mythbusters: About the Show," Discovery Channel, dsc.discovery.com/fansites/mythbusters/about/about.html.

7. To obtain this series, go to www.churchandculture.org/media.asp and scroll down to "Mythbusting."

Chapter 22 Listening to the Unchurched

1. Philip Yancey, *The Jesus I Never Knew* (Grand Rapids: Zondervan, 1995), 147–48.

2. For more information on how people view the church, see David Kinnaman and Gabe Lyons, *Unchristian: What a New Generation Really Thinks about Christianity* (Grand Rapids: Baker, 2007). See also David Van Biema, "Christianity's Image Problem," October 2, 2007, *Time U.S.*; online at http://www.time.com/time/nation/article/0,8599,1667639,00.html.

3. Kinnaman and Lyons, 34.

4. Carl Richards, "Self-Delusion on Finances," *New York Times*, October 29, 2011, B4.

Chapter 23 No Longer Seeking

1. Grossman, "'Nones' Now 15%."

2. Jonathan Rauch, "Let It Be," *Atlantic Monthly*, May 2003, 34.

3. Cathy Lynn Grossman, "God? Religion? Atheism? Millions Shrug 'So What?'" *USA Today*, December 25, 2011; online at http://www.usatoday.com/news/religion/story/2011-12-25/religion-god-atheism-so-what.

4. Thom S. Rainer, *The Unchurched Next Door: Understanding Faith Stages* (Grand Rapids: Zondervan, 2003), 24.

5. Adelle M. Banks, "U.S. Churches Still Losing Members," *Charlotte Observer*, Religion News Service, October 8, 2011; online at http://www.charlotteobserver.com/2011/10/08/2670092/us-churches-still-losing-members.html#storylink=misearch.

6. This report can be found at faithcommunitiestoday.org/decade-change.

7. "Catholic Church in India Says Have More Children," Fox News, October 10, 2011; online at http://www.foxnews.com/world/2011/10/11/catholic-church-in-india-says-have-more-children/?test=latestnews.

8. Rauch, "Let It Be," 34.

Chapter 24 Clash of Civilizations

1. From "Where Were You (When the World Stopped Turning)," words and music by Alan Jackson. © 2001 EMI APRIL MUSIC INC. and TRI-ANGELS MUSIC INC. All rights

controlled and administered by EMI APRIL MUSIC INC. All rights reserved. International copyright secured. Used by permission of Hal Leonard Corporation.

2. Cahill, *How the Irish Saved Civilization*, 3.

3. Ibid., 194.

4. John L. Allen, Jr. *The Future Church: How Ten Trends Are Revolutionizing the Catholic Church* (New York: Doubleday, 2009), 96.

5. The "Muslim Demographics" video can be seen online at http://www.youtube.com/watch?v=6-3X5hIFXYU.

6. Robert Parham, "Anti-Muslim Immigration Video Spreads Fear, Distorts Truth," *Ethics Daily*, May 11, 2009; online at http://www.ethicsdaily.com/news.php?viewStory=14194.

7. Pew Forum on Religion and Public Life 2011 study, "The Future of the Global Muslim Population," cited in *USA Today*, July 25, 2011, 2A.

8. "Muslim Mosques Growing at a Rapid Pace in the US," Faith Communities Today, December 6, 2001, http://faithcommunitiestoday.org/muslim-mosques-growing-rapid-pace-us.

9. Samuel P. Huntington, *The Clash of Civilizations and the Remaking of World Order* (New York: Simon and Schuster, 1996).

10. Findings from the Pew Forum on Religion and Public Life, reported by the *Los Angeles Times*, "Christianity Has Become Less European Over Past Century, Study Says," December 19, 2011; online at http://latimesblogs.latimes.com/world_now/2011/12/christianity-less-european-study-says.html.

11. "Christians and Lions," *The Economist*, December 31, 2011, 9.

12. Christopher Weber, "Lowe's Pulls Ads from Muslim Show, Draws Fire," *Charlotte Observer*, December 12, 2011.

13. Timothy George, "Is the God of Muhammad the Father of Jesus?" *Christianity Today*, February 4, 2002, 6–7.

14. Philip Yancey, *What's So Amazing about Grace?* (Grand Rapids: Zondervan, 1997), 45.

Chapter 25 Whatever Happened to Evangelism?

1. Tony Campolo, *Let Me Tell You a Story: Life Lessons from Unexpected Places and Unlikely People* (Nashville: Thomas Nelson, 2000), 108.

2. T. S. Eliot, *Christianity and Culture* (Orlando, FL: Harcourt, 2008), 47.

3. Penn Jillette, "Penn Says: A Gift of a Bible," *Crackle*, December 8, 2008, http://crackle.com/c/Penn_Says/A_Gift_of_a_Bible/2415037. Used by permission.

Afterword

1. For Coupland's pessimism, see http://www.theglobeandmail.com/news/national/a-radical-pessimists-guide-to-the-next-10-years/article1750609/singlepage.

2. Kevin Roberts, "Choosing Optimism," *Connect*, October 26, 2010, http://krconnect.blogspot.com/2010/10/choosing-optimism.html.

3. Richard Landes, "On Owls, Roosters, and Apocalyptic Time: A Historical Method for Reading a Refractory Documentation," *Union Seminary Quarterly Review* 49, no. 1–2 (1996), cited by Robert G. Clouse, Robert N. Hosack, and Richard V. Pierard, *The New Millennium Manual: A Once and Future Guide* (Grand Rapids: Baker, 1999), 12.

4. Clouse, Hosack, and Pierard, *The New Millennium Manual*, 12.

James Emery White, PhD, is the founding and senior pastor of Mecklenburg Community Church in Charlotte, North Carolina; president of Serious Times, a ministry that explores the intersection of faith and culture; ranked adjunctive professor of theology and culture at Gordon-Conwell Theological Seminary, which he also served as their fourth president; and author of over a dozen books that have been translated into ten languages. You can read his blog at www.churchandculture.org and follow him on Twitter @JamesEmeryWhite.

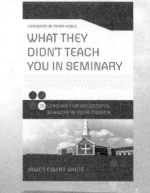

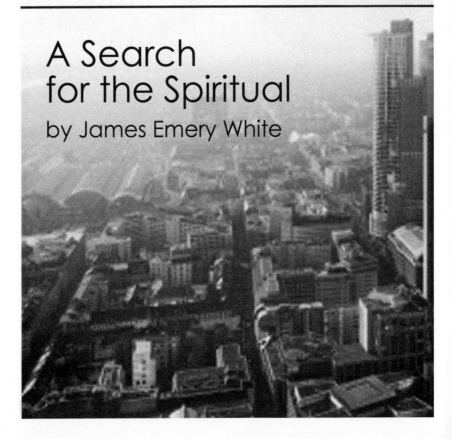

"I wish this book had been around when I was an atheist and started to seek God. It's a no-nonsense, practical, insightful guide that will help all seekers in their quest for spiritual truth. If you're investigating whether there's any substance to the Christian faith, you must read this important book."

—**Lee Strobel,** author, *The Case for Christ*

"If you've been looking for one book to put in the hands of someone exploring faith, this is it."

—**Bill Hybels,** senior pastor,
Willow Creek Community Church

A Search for the Spiritual
by James Emery White

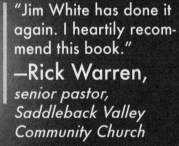

"This book is a rich blend of thoughtful, biblical reflection and hands-on experience. It will make an enormous contribution to the lives of those who believe that the local church is the hope of the world."
—**Bill Hybels**, senior pastor, Willow Creek Community Church

Rethinking
the
Church

by James Emery White

"Jim White has done it again. I heartily recommend this book."
—**Rick Warren**, *senior pastor, Saddleback Valley Community Church*